Make Your Own Maps

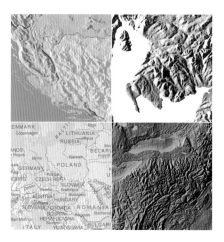

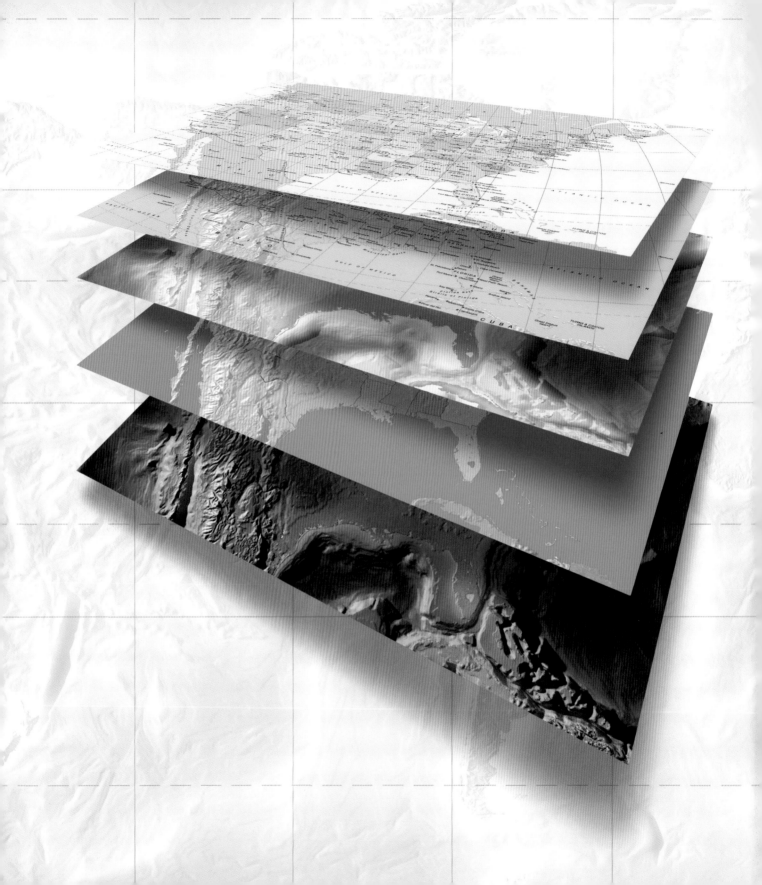

Graham Davis

Make Your Own Maps

160 COLOR MAPS READY TO PERSONALIZE ON YOUR COMPUTER

STERLING

New York / London
www.sterlingpublishing.com

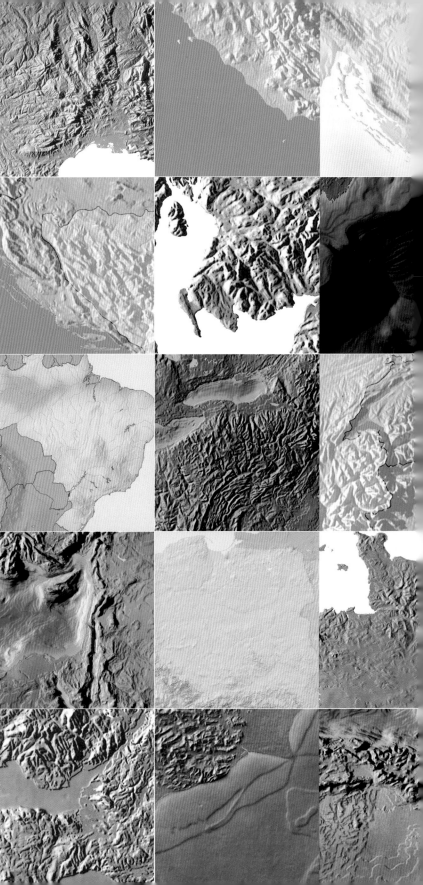

Library of Congress Cataloging-in-Publication
Data Available

1 2 3 4 5 6 7 8 9 10

Published in 2008 by Sterling Publishing Co., Inc.
387 Park Avenue South, New York, NY 10016

Copyright © 2008 The Ilex Press Limited
Maps copyright © 2008 Digital Wisdom, Inc.

Distributed in Canada by Sterling Publishing
c/o Canadian Manda Group, 165 Dufferin Street
Toronto, Ontario, Canada M6K 3H6

For information about custom editions, special sales,
premium and corporate purchases, please contact
Sterling Special Sales Department at 800-805-5489
or specialsales@sterlingpub.com

Manufactured in China

Sterling ISBN-13: 978-1-4027-5247-6
 ISBN-10: 1-4027-5247-4

Introduction

INTRODUCTION

WHAT YOU CAN DO WITH MAPS

There are 160 maps on the *Make Your Own Maps* DVD, covering the entire world. They have been created both for ease of use and for adaptability. You can use them as they are are, or you can augment them by adding your own graphics, photos, or text. The maps are ideally suited to home or academic use; they all fit within a Letter/A4 size and will print perfectly using a regular desktop printer.

So let's look at what you might do with them:

For home use:
- ☐ Create a reminder of a vacation using a map, some photos, and a special effect title; this could be used as the cover of a calendar as well.
- ☐ Make a memento of the military exploits of a relative using a sepia photo, a scanned medal, and a map of the area in which they served.
- ☐ Create a personal travel record, identify the places you have visited and the dates that you were there.

For academic use:
- ☐ Print out a map with the capital city text removed but the dots still visible, use as a "name the capital city" quiz.
- ☐ Use a combination of maps to show the Age of Discovery, Columbus, Magellan, Cook, etc. Add the routes and flags.
- ☐ Use various maps to show how climate change might affect desert growth, sea level rise, etc.
- ☐ Use the world map and add an overlay to show areas where the major religions dominate.

The maps are supplied in Photoshop/Photoshop Elements (.PSD) format and can be saved in JPEG, or other popular formats for just about any software application.

The tutorials in the book have been based on Adobe's popular Photoshop Elements image editing software, which will allow you to manipulate the maps in any number of ways to suit your purpose. They will also work in other image editing software that uses layers and can read .PSD files, but if you don't have anyhting suitable you can download a free trial of the latest version of Photoshop Elements at www.adobe.com.

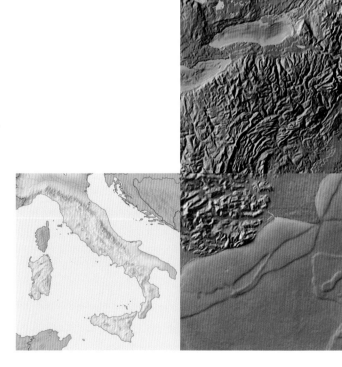

Adobe Photoshop Elements, despite being a much cheaper product than the full version of Photoshop, retains the majority of the features included in its big brother. For the novice it is also much easier to use. Adobe has seen fit to update the Microsoft Windows version to 5 while the Mac version is still at 4. Although there are some additional features in version 5 and a change to the interface styling, all the core features used in this book are available in both versions. The purpose of this chapter is to get you up and running as quickly as possible, however, if you are already an experienced Elements user, you may want to go straight to How to Use the Maps (see page 24).

So what is Photoshop Elements and what does it do? It is an image editor; you can manipulate or combine existing images or create new ones using an array of tools, filters, and effects. You can retouch and improve photos. You can make photo creations using the automated templates. You can add text to your creations using the fonts installed on your computer. As you can see, it is very versatile but there are a few things it cannot do. It cannot preview images in CMYK (the colors used in printing), so some screen colors may not print accurately. It does not have draggable guides to help position content. Its text handling is limited: you cannot use tracking to space out text, use tabs to align text, or control the space between paragraphs; but these are minor shortcomings compared with the power that it offers.

At the heart of that power is its use of layers (see page 10-11). When you create a new document it only has a background, you can then add a new layer each time you draw or paint in what Elements calls the "active image area". If you add text or use the Paste command, a new layer is automatically created. You can apply an effect to one layer without affecting the others, and add as many layers as you like.

Each map on the DVD is supplied with multiple layers, and on the following pages we have concentrated on techniques that enable you to get the best out of them. They include altering color, adding additional text and graphics, and applying special effects.

7

Adobe **Photoshop Elements** 5.0 — Online Tutorial and Videos

 Product Overview

 View and Organize Photos

 Quickly Fix Photos

 Edit and Enhance Photos

Make Photo Creations

Play Ball!

Edit and Enhance Photos

- Fine tune exposure with Color Curves variations.
- Instantly convert color photos into rich black and whites.
- Easily correct camera lens distortion.
- Sharpen blurred edges and get crisper photos.
- Use Layer Styles to add drop shadows, glows and even textures to text and shapes.
- Perfect and trasform your photos with the full array of editing tools and palettes.
- Add text, graphics, and artistic effects.
- Brush away flaws and wrinkles with the Spot Healing Brush.
- Use layers to create composite images.
- Create a panorama with Photomerge.

PART 1 · BASIC PHOTOSHOP TECHNIQUES

FINDING YOUR WAY AROUND THE INTERFACE

Adobe has taken pains to make Photoshop Elements user friendly, so the interface is structured around a range of tasks and it is easy to swap from one to another. When you open Elements 5 for the first time you are offered a range of options (version 4 is very similar):

□ Product Overview
□ View and Organize Photos
□ Quickly Fix Photos
□ Edit and Enhance Photos
□ Make Photo Creations

You can select whether to see this screen every time you open Elements, or to open directly into the Editor or Organizer next time. The Editor will be the module used most often in this book as it contains the tools that will be used to change color, add graphics or text, etc. The Organizer allows you to group together the images that you have created in order to use them in the Create module, which includes albums, calendars, slide shows, etc. When you save your creation, Elements gives you the option to Include in the Organizer or not. Regardless of your choice only the single file is saved, but if the Organizer contains a lot of images and you are using a slightly older computer, it can slow things down a bit. If you choose not to add your creations to the Organizer when you save, you can add them later.

The annotated interface screens show the Elements 5 version for Windows, and the Elements 4 for Mac. Both include a Palette Bin to the right and a Photo Bin at the bottom and when you click on them they either collapse to give you more work space, or fly out so you can access their content. All open files are shown in the Photo Bin, including the maps. On the left side of the screen is the vertical Tools palette. Whenever a particular tool is selected, additional functions for it are displayed in the Options Bar toward the top of the screen. Many tool icons have a small arrow indicating a flyout menu with alternate variants of the tool. The palettes in the Palette Bin can be "torn off" if you prefer to position them elsewhere in your workspace. Above the Options Bar are the Shortcut icons, and above that, the Menu Bar. The Quick Fix button is intended solely for improving photos.

When you open a map or any other image it appears in the active image area; you can zoom in and out of it using either the Zoom Tool or using the keyboard shortcut Ctrl/Cmd +, or Ctrl/Cmd -. When working on an image that you have zoomed into, the % enlargement is shown bottom left. When it is 100% the image is shown at its actual pixel size, so you can evaluate its real image quality. When you open a map, the size it appears on screen will be dependent on your monitor/screen size. Typically, to fit the entire map, the zoom will be about 50%.

PHOTOSHOP ELEMENTS 5
Elements 5 is currently only available for Windows PCs, but like earlier versions Adobe has gone to great lengths to make it as user friendly as possible.

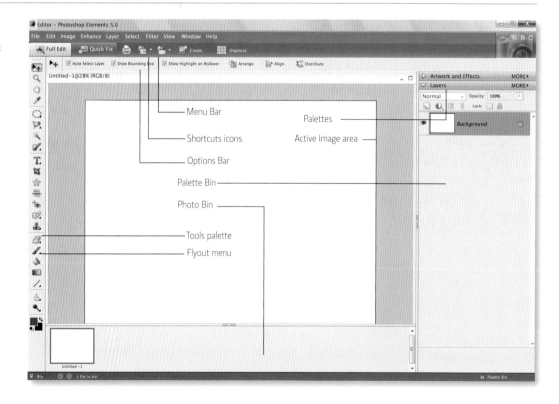

- Menu Bar
- Shortcuts icons
- Options Bar
- Palettes
- Active Image area
- Palette Bin
- Photo Bin
- Tools palette
- Flyout menu

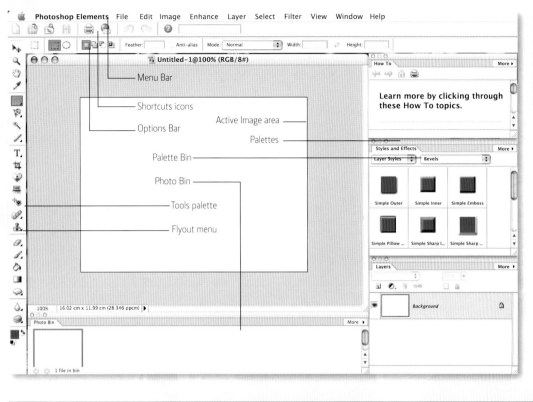

Menu Bar

Shortcuts icons

Options Bar

Active Image area

Palettes

Palette Bin

Photo Bin

Tools palette

Flyout menu

PHOTOSHOP ELEMENTS 4

If you're a Mac user then Adobe Photoshop Elements 4 is the latest version available. It lacks some of the features of Elements 5, but still provides everything you need to edit the maps.

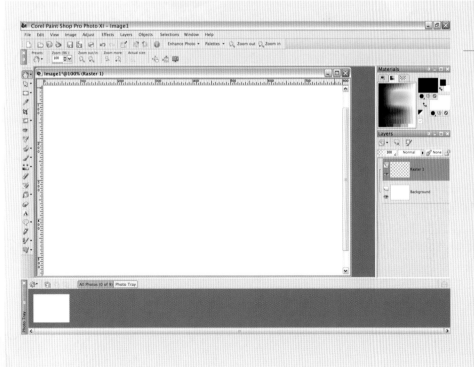

AN ALTERNATIVE TO PHOTOSHOP ELEMENTS

You can open the maps using a rival application like Corel Paint Shop Pro, which contains many similar features to Elements, and is also modestly priced. The layers will remain intact, but some of the terminology will be different, particularly when applying effects to layers. If you are lucky enough to have a full version of Photoshop then you will find the instructions in this book correspond with many of the features that you are used to. Unlike Photoshop though, Elements previews your image in RGB whereas Photoshop can preview it in CMYK as well, giving you a more accurate impression of how an image will print.

USING LAYERS

The Layers Palette is the "control panel" of any Photoshop Elements image. The easiest way to think of layers is as clear sheets of acetate placed over the background. Unlike a conventional artist you can paint the sky on one layer, the foreground on another, trees on another, and perhaps a figure on yet another. You can then make changes to each layer independently of the others. Each layer is initially opaque, but by changing the opacity of a layer you can allow a little of the layer below to show through. You can even change the way the layers blend together. Fortunately, even for the novice, using layers is quite straightforward once you understand the basics.

Before you make any changes to a layer you must click on it in the Layers Palette; it then becomes the active layer. Elements also allows you to click on the active image area to select a layer, this is convenient if you have an image where the elements on each layer are clearly separate, like a montage of photos; however this is not the case with the maps. You can turn this feature on or off using Auto Select Layer on the menu bar.

THE BACKGROUND

When you create a new Elements document it consists of just the Background. Although you can draw or paint directly on to it, it is better to keep it blank and create a new Layer to work on; the benefits will become clear during this chapter.

DUPLICATING LAYERS

To duplicate a layer, either drag the layer and drop it onto the Create New Layer icon, or select Duplicate Layer from the More button in the Layers palette. To rename the new layer, right mouse click on a PC, or Option/Click on a Mac.

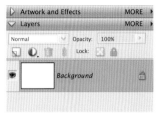

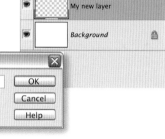

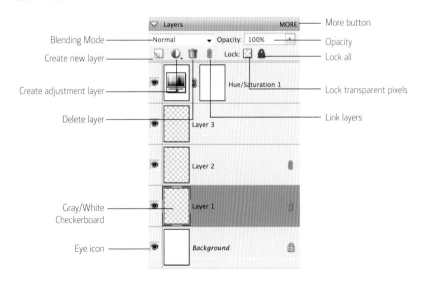

Blending Mode
Create new layer
Create adjustment layer
Delete layer
Gray/White Checkerboard
Eye icon

More button
Opacity
Lock all
Lock transparent pixels
Link layers

Hue/Saturation 1
Layer 3
Layer 2
Layer 1
Background

BLENDING MODE
Shows how each layer blends with the ones below. The default is Normal.

OPACITY
Indicates how much of the layers below will show through.

CREATE A NEW LAYER
Adds a new layer above the current active layer. You can also duplicate a layer by dragging it onto the icon.

CREATE AN ADJUSTMENT LAYER
This special layer is used to alter the layers below it. Commonly used to change color (Hue/Saturation).

DELETE LAYER
Deletes the active layer.

LINK LAYERS
When multiple layers are selected this links them together. Move one, and they all move.

LOCK TRANSPARENT PIXELS
This stops you from painting over the edge of the image on that layer.

LOCK ALL
Locks the active layer so you cannot make any changes to it.

The **gray/white checkerboard** indicates that this area is transparent.

The **Eye icon** indicates layer visibility.

The **More** button prompts a flyout menu with additional controls. Most are self-evident, but some are grayed out initially and will be dealt with later in this chapter. The two Merge options and Flatten Image are best avoided, as you will no longer be able to edit layers individually. The Palette Options allow you to change the size of the icons, or even hide them altogether.

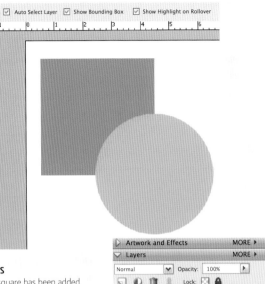
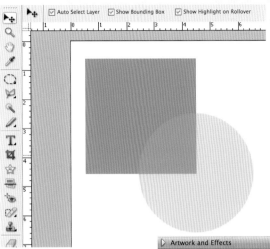
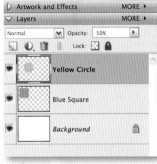

BASIC LAYERS

Here a blue square has been added on a new Layer, followed by a yellow circle on another Layer above it. By default, the Opacity of each layer is 100%, so the circle obscures part of the square below it.

LAYER OPACITY

Here the Opacity of the yellow circle layer has been reduced to 50%. It becomes a paler color and the blue square shows through from the layer below.

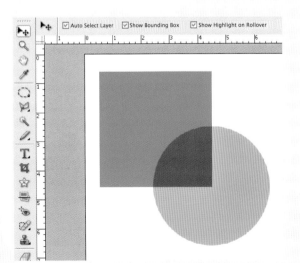
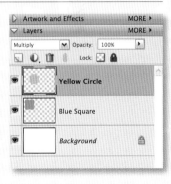

BLENDING MODES

Here the yellow circle layer Opacity has been restored to 100%, but the Blending Mode has been changed to Multiply. This allows the blue square to show through without the yellow circle becoming paler.

USING MASKS

Photoshop Elements has several tools for masking an area of the active layer. When masked, only the area within the mask can be altered. To modify the area outside the mask you will need to select Inverse from the Select menu. This menu also offers the option of selecting All, which means the entire area of that layer. Elements refers to these masks as Selections. To create a selection, use the Rectangular Marquee or the Elliptical Marquee tool found in the Tools palette (the latter as a flyout option). Holding the mouse button down, drag the cursor over the area required and release; the

selection is indicated by what is popularly referred to as "marching ants," because the selection becomes an animated broken line. If you want the selection to be a perfect square or circle, then hold the Shift key down as you drag the cursor. You can also make a selection on an empty layer and fill it with color using the Paint Bucket tool. The area will be filled with the current foreground color, so you need to select this color before you proceed.

SAVING SELECTIONS

Choose a tool and then draw the area to be selected. If you want to save it for future use, choose Save Selection from the Select menu, and give it a name.

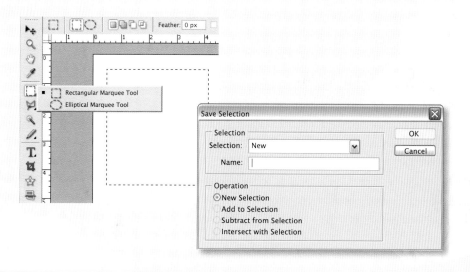

FEATHERING SELECTIONS

Once a selection has been made there is another option available—Feather. This vignettes the edge of the selection, so when filled with a color, the edge is softened, fading gradually to full transparency. You will need to use trial and error when setting the Feather Radius.

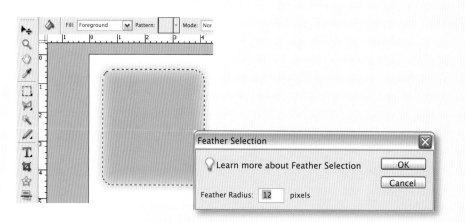

ADDING BORDERS

Choosing the Border option from the Select menu puts an outline—or "stroke"— around the edge of the selection using the currently selected Foreground color. The thickness here is 6 pixels and centered on the Selection.

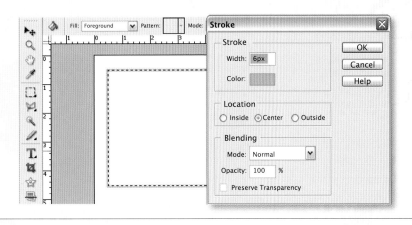

EXPAND, CONTRACT, GROW AND SIMILAR

Expand and Contract are self-explanatory—they increase or decrease the size of the selection. Grow selection means that it expands to fill adjacent pixels of the same color, while Similar adds any pixels of the same color to the selection, even if they are not adjacent. The Tolerance setting allows you to vary the degree of these effects, but unfortunately you cannot preview the result until you have either filled the selection with color, or used it to remove part of an existing layer.

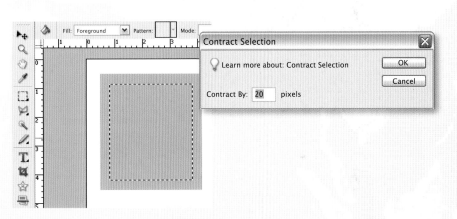

THE COOKIE CUTTER

The Cookie Cutter tool includes a variety of shape options; when you have selected one, click and drag it over the image area. When you release the mouse, the image outside the area is deleted.

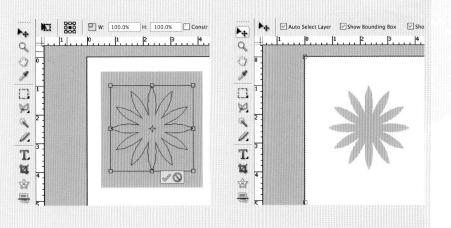

MAKING SELECTIONS

In addition to the basic methods of making a selection, Elements provides several other, more advanced techniques. The Magic Wand tool is usually used to identify an area around which you want to make a selection, for example a building in front of a blue sky. Click on the sky with the Magic Wand tool and a selection will appear around the building. An alternative method is to use the Magnetic Lasso tool. Select it from the Tools palette, position it close to the edge of the area you want to select and, holding the mouse button down, run the cursor along the edge. You will see that

the selection that you are making attempts to cling to the edge. You must bring the cursor back to where you started and double click to complete the selection. However, there is a problem with both these methods, as they rely on changes in color to identify the edge that separates the two parts of the image, and even sky is rarely a flat blue. There is a third method available in Elements 5 and that is the Magic Extractor, as described below.

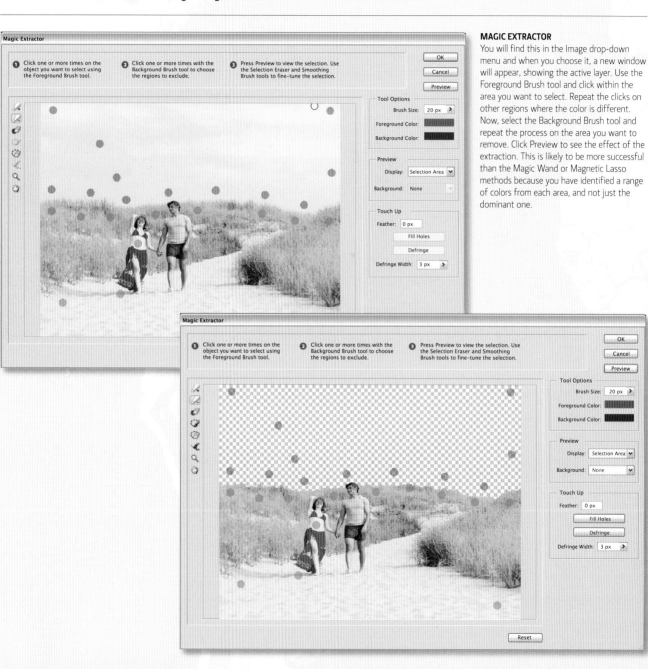

MAGIC EXTRACTOR

You will find this in the Image drop-down menu and when you choose it, a new window will appear, showing the active layer. Use the Foreground Brush tool and click within the area you want to select. Repeat the clicks on other regions where the color is different. Now, select the Background Brush tool and repeat the process on the area you want to remove. Click Preview to see the effect of the extraction. This is likely to be more successful than the Magic Wand or Magnetic Lasso methods because you have identified a range of colors from each area, and not just the dominant one.

LASSO TOOLS

If all else fails you can always "trace" around the area using the Freehand or Polygonal Lasso tools. Zoom in on the area you want to select and use a steady hand with the Freehand Lasso, or a multitude of small steps with the Polygonal Lasso to follow the shape. Move the cursor back to where you started to complete the selection.

MODIFYING SELECTIONS

When you use any of the selection tools, you will notice the icons that appear in the Options Bar offer further alternatives: Add to selection; Subtract from selection; and Intersect with selection. These can be useful if you want to make a change to a selection.

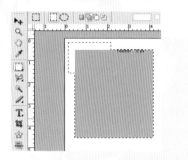

CUSTOM SHAPE TOOL

The Custom Shape tool can be used to create both regular and custom shape selections. Although it is similar to the Cookie Cutter, a new Shape Layer is created, filled with the current Foreground color, rather than the shape being cut out of an existing layer.Because the Shape Layer is a vector graphic (not a bitmap image) it can be scaled without any loss of quality. The Shape Layer appears within a gray rectangle on the Layers Palette. To create a selection from it you must first select Simplify using the More button; this converts it to a bitmap so you can now use the Magic Wand to create the selection.

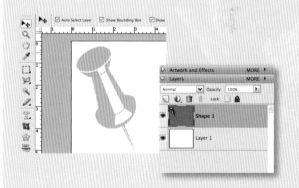

TIP

As an alternative to using the Magic Wand tool, Ctrl/Cmd-Click the layer thumbnail of a layer that includes some transparent areas, to create a selection.

Drawing and painting tools

16

DRAWING AND PAINTING TOOLS

Elements has extensive drawing and painting tools that include both the standard Brush and Pencil tools. These are available in a wide range of alternative types and sizes that can be chosen from the Options Bar after a brush or pencil has been selected. In addition to these, the Impressionist Brush adds a variety of exotic effects to an image by brushing over it. The Color Replacement tool, although it is a brush, is not really a painting tool as it is used to replace an area of color with the current foreground color, when you brush over it. As well as painting with a brush, you can fill an area with a color using the Paint Bucket tool. The Tolerance setting is very important here, as it determines how similar colors need to be to be replaced. The higher the tolerance, the closer they have to be to the target colour to be replaced, and unless it is a completely flat color the Paint Bucket is unlikely to fill the area that you intended. If this is the case use the "Replace Color" method described on page 19. Finally, the Gradient tool combines the foreground and background colors to create a smooth blend.

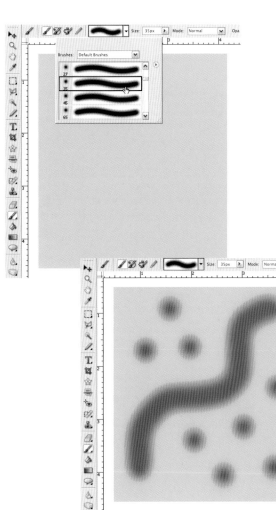

BRUSHES
There are a wide range of Brushes and Pens available and all are customizable. Here, a Soft Round 35 pixel brush has been used; the soft edge blends with the blue rectangle on the layer below.

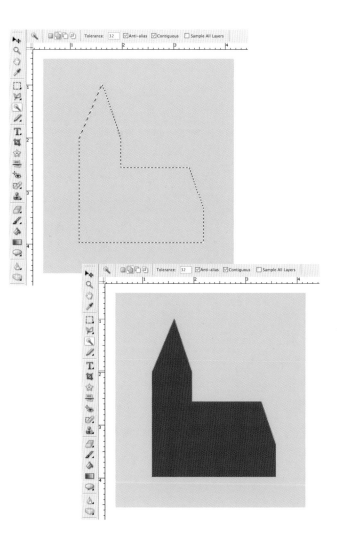

SIMPLE SILHOUETTES
Drawing and painting can benefit from the use of selections. For example, if you want to create a silhouette of a church it is easiest to define the shape using the Polygonal Lasso tool, and then fill with color using the Paint Bucket tool.

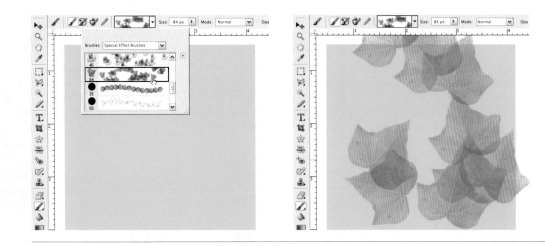

SPECIAL EFFECT BRUSHES

The Special Effect Brushes offer a huge range of customizable alternatives. You can paint using a brush loaded with "Falling Ivy Leaves", for example, and the choices appear in the Options Bar when this tool is selected. Remember to select the foreground color before you commence painting.

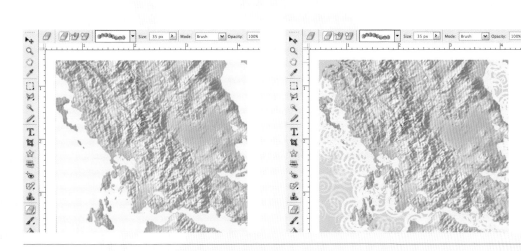

ERASER

The Eraser tool is also a brush, and is intended for correction, but it can also be used creatively. For example, painting out areas of an image using the Hypno Lines brush will reveal those areas on the layer beneath. The Options Bar allows you to control the brush size and opacity settings.

PAINT BUCKET

Before you use the Paint Bucket tool, make a selection to define the area that you want to fill, then click on the Color Picker to select a color. Finally, click within the selection to flood it with color.

GRADIENTS

Before you use the Gradient tool, make sure that you have selected both a foreground and a background color. The Options Bar shows a thumbnail image of the gradient as well as alternative types of gradient like Radial, and Reflected.

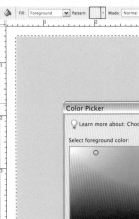

CHANGING COLOR

The ability to change the color of an image is one of Elements' major strengths and it can be done in either of two ways: overall or selective. The most direct way to change the overall color is to select Adjust Color from the Enhance drop-down menu, and then select Hue/Saturation. You can then use sliders to change the color. If you check the Colorize option a monochrome tint is applied—this is particularly useful if you have a black-and-white image and you want to add a color to it. To selectively replace a color, choose Replace Color from the Enhance menu. Click on the Color swatch in the Selection part of the window, and use the Eyedropper tool to sample the color that you want to replace. Finally, use the sliders to change the color. You can also create an adjustment layer. This is found in the Layers palette and adds a special editable layer above the active one that enables you to change the Hue/Saturation, as well as several other image characteristics, without permanently altering your original image. If you make a selection prior to creating it, only this area will change color.

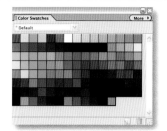

COLOR SWATCHES

If you choose a color that you want to reuse on another project, you can add it to the Swatch palette, available from Color Swatches in the Window drop down menu. Use the Create New Color Swatch button, give it a name, and the current foreground color will be saved permanently.

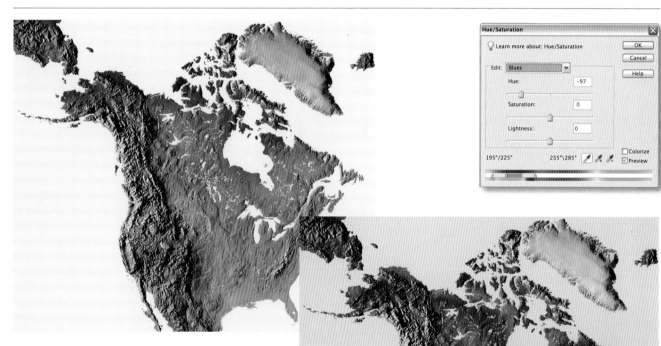

COLOR

Changing the Hue/Saturation values overall can yield some surprising results, as all the colors in an image change when you drag the sliders back and forth. The Edit drop-down menu enables you to change specific color ranges, while the default Master option changes all of them together. Here, Blues has been selected from the Edit menu and the Hue slider dragged to -97.

Changing color

18

REPLACE COLOR

The Replace Color palette has two controls. Selection allows you to select the color that you want to replace, and adjusting the Fuzziness slider will vary the area affected. Use the hue, saturation and lightness controls in the Replacement panel to select the new color by dragging the sliders.

POSTERIZE

Click on the Create an Adjustment Layer icon in the Layers palette and select Posterize. In the resulting Levels dialog, lower values will produce a more exaggerated result.

SCREEN COLOR

Not all colors will print exactly as they appear on screen, so some are best avoided. Open the Color Picker and drag the round picker cursor to the extreme right of the color display. Now change the R/G/B values to 0/255/0 and compare the bright green on screen with the green printed in this book—it is much less vibrant. Now try 0/255/255 and compare the turquoise to the book. These two colors—and those that are close to them—are a problem, because a printer has to convert screen colors (RGB) to ones that can be printed (CMYK).

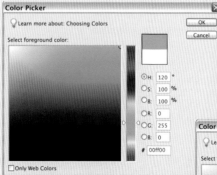

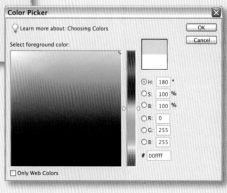

THE TEXT TOOLS

In Elements 5, there are two initial options when adding type. The first is to click in the active image area (which creates a new Text Layer), and start typing. The resulting type will use the font, size, color, and alignment shown in the Options Bar. Don't worry, as all these can be changed later. Unless you hit the Return key the type will be set to Single Line.

The second method is to click and hold the mouse button down as you drag the cursor down and right. When you release the mouse button a text frame will appear, which allows you to type Paragraph Text that fills the frame. If you need more space, simply drag out the frame to accommodate it. You will only be able to use fonts that are installed on your computer, but as they are on their own layer they will remain editable. If you plan to share this document with a friend, they may not have the same fonts as you. The solution is to right mouse click (or select More from the layers palette) and select Simplify Layer. This converts the layer into a bitmap image, making the font unnecessary. You can also save the bitmap file in JPEG format, but this will flatten all the layers.

INSTALLING FONTS

Both Windows PCs and Macs are supplied with a small number of fonts. More are available online, and many of them are free (see page 144). When you have acquired additional fonts they will need to be installed before you can use them. On a Windows PC select **Start** > **Control Panel** > **Fonts** and select Install from the File menu. On a Mac select **Library Folder** > **Fonts**, and drag them into it.

TEXT LEADING

Use Set the Leading from the Options Bar to control the space between lines of type. "Leading" owes its name to the thin strips of lead that were placed between lines of type in the days before computerized type setting and points. Here it has been increased to 60 pt.

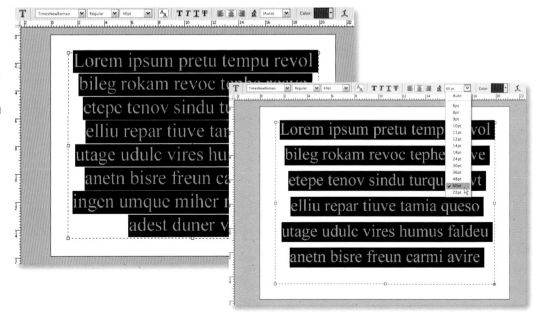

20

ANTI-ALIASED TEXT

The Anti-aliased button on the Options Bar toggles between on (the default setting), and off. If you zoom in on some text at 800% and click the button, you will see the difference. Without anti-aliasing, the curved letters look jagged as the letterforms are actually made up of tiny rectangular steps (pixels).

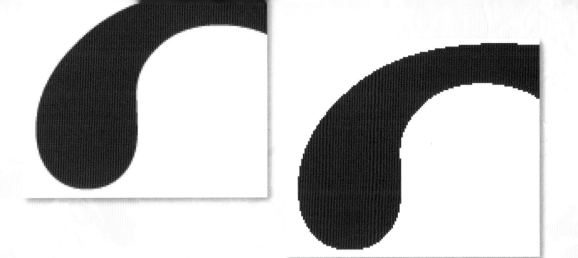

TYPE MASK TOOL

Instead of setting text as type, you can use the Horizontal or Vertical Type Mask tool to create a selection. This is useful if you want the text to be cut out of an image, or filled with a pattern. You can achieve the same result by using the Magic Wand to create a selection on an existing type layer.

WARPED TEXT

When you have created a Text Layer you can use Create Warped Text from the Options Bar to produce a range of distortions. The text remains editable and you can reverse the process by selecting None from the menu. Each warp effect has a series of slider controls to enable adjustments to be made.

FILTERS, STYLES, AND EFFECTS

Elements 5 now includes Artwork and Themes in addition to the Filters, Styles, and Effects of version 4. They can be located in the Artwork and Effects palette, or the Styles and Effects palette respectively. The layer styles can be applied to both text and graphics layers, whilst the text effects apply only to text. The application of either one will add an icon to the layer that can be clicked to offer additional options. In Elements 4 some of these options are grayed out, whereas in version 5 they are fully editable. The remaining effects—and all the filters—can only be applied to graphic layers, unless you simplify a text layer first. When you apply some texture

effects it adds a new effect layer, which will appear above the active layer in Elements 4 so you may need to drag it down the layer stack to make other layers visible. In Elements 5 these effects are applied to the background, so you may have to duplicate the background layer and delete the original to move the Texture layer to the bottom of the layer stack.

LAYER STYLES AND SIZE

The appearance of a Layer Style is dependent on the size of the object that it is being applied to; on a small item of type, for example, it may be unnoticeable, or only barely visible. Click on the Layer Style icon and see if any adjustments make a difference. If not, either try another style or increase the size of the object.

WOW NEON

This layer style is called Wow Neon and has been applied to a simple sans serif font. In Elements 4 some of the options are grayed out, whilst in version 5 they are all editable. If you open styles applied in Elements 4, in the full version of Photoshop they will become fully editable.

TIP

There are so many Artwork and Effects settings that it's worth hitting the Add to Favorites button when you find one you use often. This will make it much easier to find in the future.

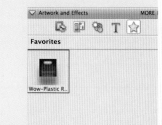

MULTIPLE LAYER STYLES

If you apply a second layer style it will override the first, so, if you want to use two or more styles, you will have to use Simplify Layer. This combines the layer with the first style and you can then apply the second style. Here a Glass Button Layer Style has been applied, the layer simplified, and then a Crystallize Filter applied.

WOW PLASTIC

Another easy way to achieve a stunning effect is to use Wow Plastic from Layer Styles, on a piece of type; it works best if the type is bold and rounded. This style is very sensitive to the size of the object, but fortunately all the slider options are available, so suitable adjustments can be made.

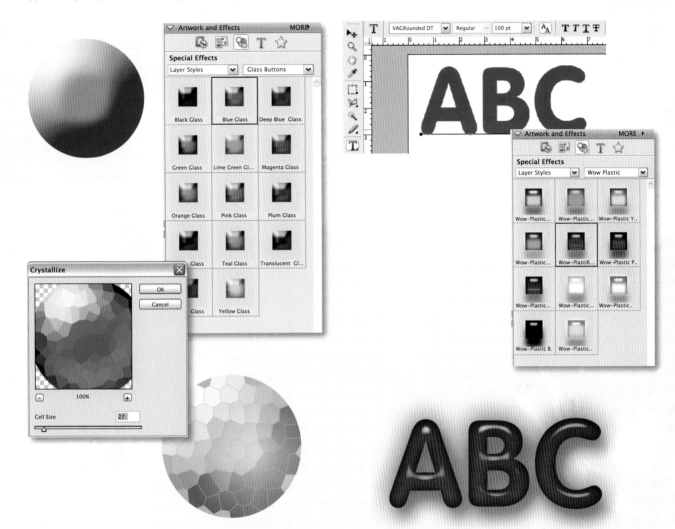

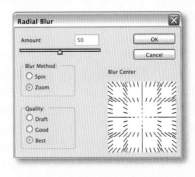

BLUR FILTERS AND STYLES

In addition to the more decorative filters and styles, there are simple ones that can be very useful, like Gaussian Blur or Motion Blur. The Radial Blur used here will apply the effect from the center of the Active Image Area, so if the object that you want to blur is off center, you will need to drag the Blur Center graphic to the correct location. You can access them from the Filter menu as well as Styles and Effects.

PART 2 · HOW TO USE THE MAPS

ABOUT THE MAP FILES

To open any of the 160 maps on the *Make Your Own Maps* DVD you will need a Windows PC or Mac with Adobe Photoshop Elements, or a similar application like PaintShop Pro or Elements' big brother, Adobe Photoshop. The content of each map is broken down into separate layers. Most maps include the standard set of layers (shown opposite), although some will have additional layers; like the State names for the USA. For other maps some layers are not necessary, for example island names for South Africa.

This chapter demonstrates the versatility of the maps and shows you how you can use combinations of layers to best effect, and how you can change the color of any layer, including text and outlines. The layers can be shown or hidden by clicking the Eye icon next to the layer's name in the Layers palette. The layer structure enables you to easily customize a map; you can create new layers adding text, photos, or graphics, or you can simply alter the existing ones using an array of effects and filters that are available to the Photoshop Elements user.

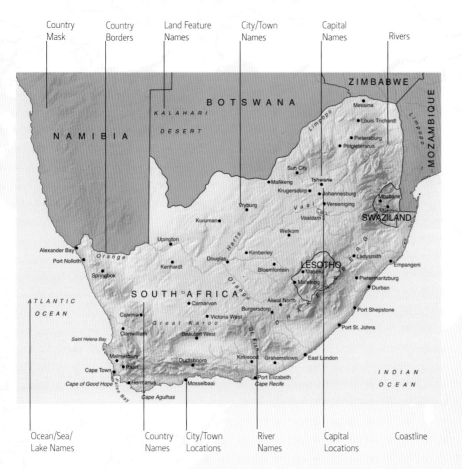

Country Mask   Country Borders   Land Feature Names   City/Town Names   Capital Names   Rivers

Ocean/Sea/ Lake Names   Country Names   City/Town Locations   River Names   Capital Locations   Coastline

MAP LAYERS

When you open the South Africa map, you will see it comprises the standard set of Layers, but without a layer for Islands. At the top of the layer stack are the Names and Location dots. The Names layers are not editable as all the text is saved as graphics files, so you don't need to worry about fonts. Below these are outline layers, for Coastline etc. Beneath these are two mask layers. The Country mask is gray and can be used to obscure the surrounding land mass, while the Water mask is black. Both can be used to isolate the country, or can be converted to a color. Below these are the two Physical layers that show topographical relief, plus the Political layer that uses color to separate surrounding countries. Finally, at the bottom is the Grayscale relief layer, which, like the mask layers, can be colored.

25

LAYERS NOT VISIBLE:
Island Names
Water Mask
Physical: Dark
Political
Grayscale

TIP

If you have made some alterations to a map but you are unable to save the changes that you have made, then you probably opened the map straight off the DVD. Save it on your computer first to avoid the problem.

LOADING AND SAVING MAP FILES

If you have enough hard disk space you can copy all the maps on the DVD to your computer. Alternatively, you can drag them off the DVD as and when you want to use them. The map files have been created to print out on an average desktop printer—for the technically minded they have a resolution of 150 ppi. They will all print at Letter/A4 paper size and we recommend you do not enlarge the maps beyond this size as the image quality will suffer.

Although the layered map files offer flexibility and allow for changes to be made at a later date, you may need a "flattened" map for use in a Microsoft Word or Publisher document (or Pages on a Mac), perhaps for a school project. Maybe you want to send it as an attachment by email, or use it on a website or social networking site like MySpace? Photoshop Elements offers a wide range of Save As options, as does Paint Shop Pro.

CANVAS SIZE

If you need some extra space around a map, select **Image Resize > Canvas Size** from the Image menu and change the Width and Height dimensions. This keeps the map central in the enlarged space. If you want to add the space to the sides, top, or bottom, click on the arrows to select. As the maps do not have a Background layer, the Canvas extension color is grayed out.

SAVE AS

When you use Save As, you must first choose the location and file name for the new file and then the format, here JPEG. Stay with the default options, particularly the Maximum Quality value of 10. Don't drop below this or the image will suffer. If you have made changes to the file, remember to Save it first.

WHICH FORMAT SHOULD I USE?

Although some applications will allow you to import a map in PSD format, many do not, and it will be necessary to use an alternative. As it is the most universal of all formats, JPG/JPEG is invariably the best choice. You can use a slider to set the image quality/file size trade off, important for web use, otherwise stick to the maximum quality setting. Is there a difference between JPG and JPEG, TIF and TIFF? No, they are the same. In the old days the PC was restricted to a three character file extension whilst the Mac was not. Formats that were developed for a particular platform—like BMP for the PC or PICT for the Mac—are now best avoided, especially if you want to share your maps with others. When you select Save As for JPG/JPEG it will save using the current resolution, which is 150 ppi for the maps. When you choose Save For Web the JPG/JPEG image is automatically changed to 72 ppi, which is the resolution appropriate for web or any other screen use. This should be avoided if the image is intended for printing.

SAVE AS	SUITABLE FOR
JPG/JPEG	All documents
TIF/TIFF	Documents intended for very high quality printing
BMP	Documents intended for printing on a PC
PICT	Documents intended for printing on a Mac

SAVE FOR WEB	SUITABLE FOR
JPEG	Web pages and online sharing
PNG and GIF	Not suitable for the map images

PHOTOSHOP ELEMENTS ORGANIZER

When you save a file in Elements you have the option to Include in Organizer. When you select this option you can then use Create to make the images into Photo Layouts and Galleries, Slide Shows, Flip Books, etc.

TIP

Don't be tempted to flatten the Elements (PSD) document. You will almost certainly regret it, because you won't be able to alter the individual layers at a later date. Instead, choose **Select All** > **Copy Merged** and then **File** > **New Image from Clipboard**. This will create a second, flattened version that you can save with a different name.

CHANGING THE MAP COLORING

The layers containing the land areas of the map have a naturalistic coloring to reflect the topography and vegetation, so it is always sensible to consider why you want to change them and plan the effect that you wish to achieve. The simplest way of changing the map color is to use Hue/Saturation to change an individual layer; other layers remain unaffected, but the change cannot be reversed. If you use a Hue/Saturation Adjustment layer, the color of all layers beneath it will change, unless you first create a mask to protect layers that you do not want to change (see page 30). This option allows you to revisit this layer later and change the color again. The Hue/Saturation options can be used in a variety of ways. If you are using several maps for a project and want to color-code the sections, Colorize is the best option, but if you want your map to have a youthful appeal try selecting a single color like yellow from the Edit menu. If you just want a very light and delicate color scheme, increasing Saturation and Lightness is the solution. On these pages are numerous options for you to try.

ADJUSTING LAND MASS COLOR

This is the default coloring of the map THE_AMERICAS. All the color variations shown on this spread use Hue/Saturation applied directly to the layer.

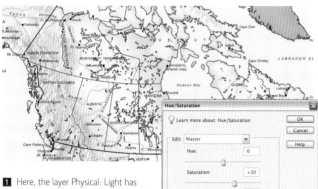

1 Here, the layer Physical: Light has been lightened further by increasing both Saturation and Lightness. The saturation is boosted so that the color does not bleach out completely.

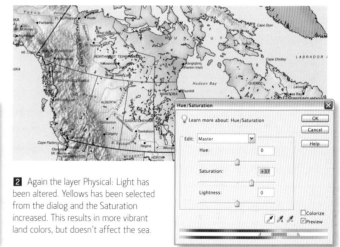

2 Again the layer Physical: Light has been altered. Yellows has been selected from the dialog and the Saturation increased. This results in more vibrant land colors, but doesn't affect the sea.

3 With the layer Physical: Light still selected, the Saturation has been increased and Lightness reduced, resulting in a much punchier color range. Reducing the Lightness on its own will result in a muddy image.

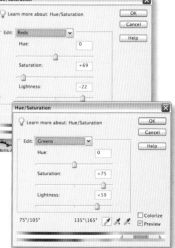

4 This time two colors in the Physical:Light layer have been adjusted. Reducing Saturation and increasing Lightness in the Reds makes the mountain relief lighter, while increasing Saturation and Lightness to the Greens makes the green fringes of the map more vibrant.

ADJUSTING WATER COLOR

1 We now turn our attention to the Water Mask layer. As it is a black mask, you must first check the Colorize button in order to add color. Increase both the Saturation and Lightness and the water areas will adopt the current Foreground color. Drag the Hue slider until you are satisfied with the color.

2 You will notice that the Water Mask Layer thumbnail has turned blue to match the new color. As it is a much darker blue, you may like to turn off the Coastline layer visibility, as the separation between sea and land is now stronger. The Opacity of both the Canadian Province Borders and USA State Borders layers has also been reduced to 40%.

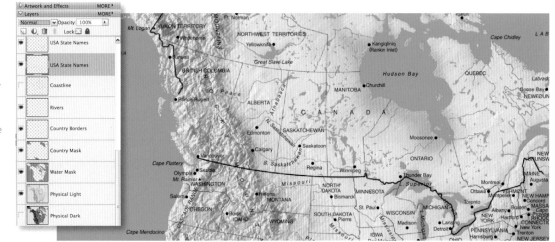

3 Using step 2 as your start point, turn off the visibility for the Physical: Light layer and turn on the Grayscale layer. Ensure that Colorize is checked, and increase both Saturation and Lightness. Drag the Hue slider to produce a suitable color; here it is a sandy yellow. Notice also that the Country Mask visibility has been turned off.

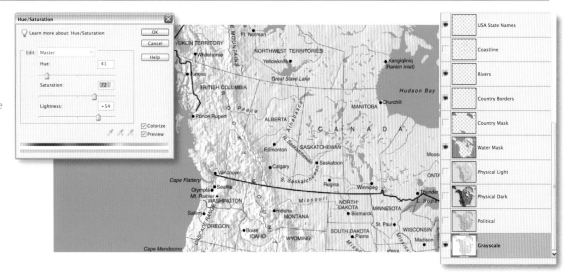

CHANGING THE MAP COLORING 2

As well as the land areas, you also can change the other layers. Take care when changing the text color to ensure that legibility is retained. It is also possible to make the text white so that it reads on a darker land or sea color. As the text is only a few pixels in width, adjusting the text is best done by making the Hue/Saturation changes directly to the layer, or to a duplicate if you think you might change your mind later on. The two mask layers offer lots of possibilities, particularly the Water Mask layer. You can make a selection using the Magic Wand tool or Ctrl/Cmd-click the layer thumbnail to create an Adjustment Layer that applies only to the land. You can save any selection so that it can be reused using the Select menu; simply give a name. When you come to load it again you will have the option to Invert it if you wish. Blending Modes can be useful when changing color, particularly the use of Multiply on a grayscale layer as it allows some of the layer below to show through, without lessening its opacity.

USING ADJUSTMENT LAYERS

1 To get the full benefit from an Adjustment Layer it needs to be masked with a selection so that it applies to a specific area. Select the Water Mask layer, and, using the Magic Wand tool, click somewhere in the transparent central area. This will create a Selection. Now click the Create adjustment layer button, select Hue/Saturation and a new layer will appear above Water Mask, which can now be turned off.

2 Double click the new adjustment layer to fire up the Hue/Saturation controls and select Reds from the Edit menu. Drag the Hue value to +25 and the Saturation to +55. Now select Yellows and drag Hue to +70, Saturation to about +36 and Lightness to +44. These values will strengthen the mountain relief and make the remaining land greener.

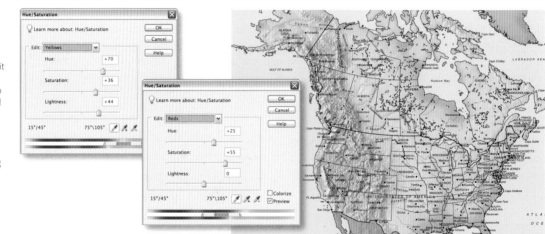

3 Now reselect the Water Mask and this time click on the black area with the Magic Wand. Turn off this layer's visibility and click on the Create adjustment layer button again. This time the new adjustment layer is a mirror image of the one created in step 2.

4 Double click the new adjustment layer to open the Hue/Saturation controls and drag the Saturation slider to -100 and the Lightness to +100. This combination reduces the sea and the lakes' color to white. Notice how the two Adjustment Layers operate independently of each other.

5 Create another adjustment layer exactly as you did for step 1, but this time turn the visibility on for Physical: Dark and off for Physical: Light. Fire up the Hue/Saturation controls and drag the Hue slider to about -27 and the Saturation and Lightness to around 60. Because Physical: Dark has denser colors, this adjustment creates a more intense result than any of the previous ones.

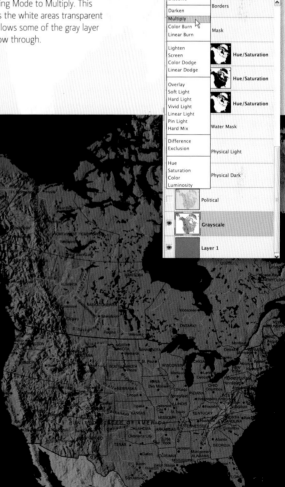

CREATING FLAT COLORS

1 When you have created a masked adjustment layer, it can be used to create flat colors. Turn off the land layers' visibility and create a new layer at the bottom of the stack, filled with a mid gray. Double click the Hue/Saturation 3 adjustment layer, check Colorize, and move the Saturation and Lightness sliders to the right. This colors the land area of the new gray layer. Drag the Hue slider to create the desired color, then repeat the process using the Hue/Saturation 2 adjustment layer to create a similar effect on the water areas.

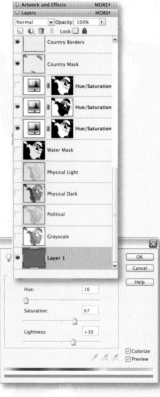

2 Turn the visibility on again for the Grayscale layer and change the Blending Mode to Multiply. This makes the white areas transparent and allows some of the gray layer to show through.

ADDING TEXT

The text on the maps is in the form of graphics, and so is not editable. The fonts used are the Arial family, preinstalled on Windows PCs and very similar to Helvetica used on Macs. You can, of course, add your own text layers to any map—either as headings or extra annotation. You can use any font installed on your computer (see page 20) and you may want to add a caption to a location name that will benefit from being set in a different font to the map names. Each time you add a piece of text to Elements a new layer is created, so it is best to use this option sparingly.

Unlike a word processor Elements does not offer a full range of text controls so it is best to limit your ambitions to suit its capabilities. Adding text will often involve creating graphics as well; for example an arrow pointing to a location, or a colored panel behind a heading. It is even possible to rescale a detail of a map to about 200 per cent if you replace the maps' text layers with your own text. The map land areas will stand this degree of enlargement, but the text will not.

SINGLE LINE TEXT

When you select the Text tool, the Options bar offers a range of settings. Here we are adding some text with additional information about a place, so we have set it a bit larger than the map text. It is set in Arial, 15 pt and ranged left. To add text to a map, first select a layer and click on the map in roughly the right place. A new text layer will appear above the layer that you selected and you can now type the text. This creates Single Line Text, not Paragraph Text. Drag the text to fine tune its position, and if you want to change the font, size, or color, you can do so in the Options bar.

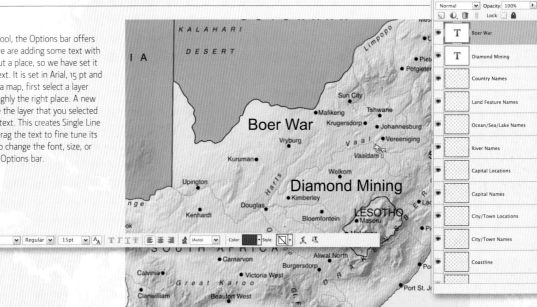

PARAGRAPH TEXT

With the Text tool selected, click and drag the cursor down and right to create a "text box." You can now type Paragraph Text. This time, the font size has been reduced to 10pt, with the title set in bold. The Country Mask visibility has been turned off to enable the new text to sit in an empty space.

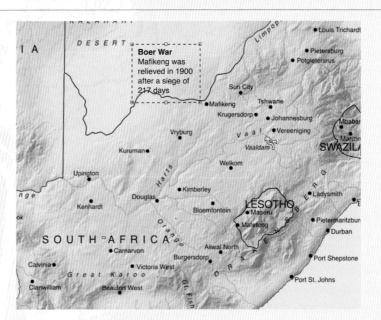

1 Adding more complex annotation is straightforward and there are some great effects like Layer Styles to aid legibility. First add the heading and six days as single line text. The days are set in 18pt Arial Bold, whilst the heading is 40pt Georgia Bold and centered rather that ranged left.

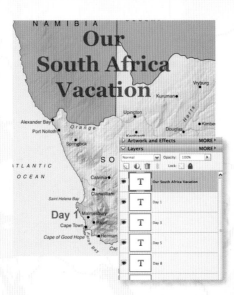

2 The Layer Country Mask normally has an Opacity value of 70%. If this is reduced to 30% it will still provide the separation of South Africa from its neighbors, but without being so intrusive. Reselect one of the new text layers and from the Artwork and Effects palette choose **Special Effects > Layer Styles > Small Border**. Make sure that only the Stroke option is checked and set Size to 6px and Opacity to 100%. This creates a black border round the text. Apply it to the other new text layers as well.

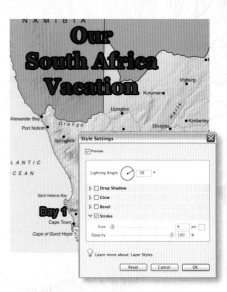

1 As well as adding text you can remove an area of existing text if you want to use the area to display a title. Here the Polygon Lasso tool has been used to surround unwanted text. Next select each of the layers in which that text occurs and delete it.

2 Once it has been deleted, select the Country Mask layer and using the Magic Wand tool click on the gray to make a selection from it. Now click the Make Adjustment Layer button and select Hue/Saturation. The Country Mask layer is no longer needed so you can turn it off using the Visibility Icon.

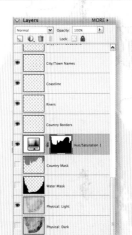

3 With the Hue/Saturation palette open, drag the Hue slider to +32 to create a green tint within the neighboring countries, move the Saturation up a bit and the Lightness down, the resulting color is subtle and some of the relief contouring shows through.

4 Now, create two text layers for the title and subtitle. Here the subtitle is set in 24pt Georgia Italic, while the title is 60pt AdLib, which has been embellished with a Text Style called Emboss. This Text Style has been used with the default setting and overrides the existing text color.

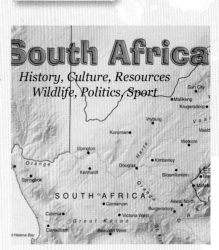

ADDING TEXT 2

Sometimes, adding text requires extending the map area as well. If the map has an extensive sea area, the obvious choice is to add to it so that extra text, graphics, or photos can be included. This can be useful if you are creating a poster, title page, or journal page. As Greece is renowned for its bright blue sea, a Hue/Saturation Adjustment Layer has been added, so that the extended sea area reflects this. It also enables the additional text to appear white, and part of the existing map text to be changed from black to white. Although Elements' basic text controls are limited, it has a fantastic feature called Create Warped Text. Not only does this offer a range of distortions—like arc, bulge, flag, squeeze and twist—but there are controls to vary the them, and all this using live text that you can edit with the distortion still applied! Combine this with a Layer Style and it is easy to create distinctive titles or even logos. You can also save the extended map without text in JPEG format, and add the text using a word processor or DTP package like MS Word or iPages.

1 In order to add text or a title to a map it is sometimes necessary to enlarge the canvas size. This doesn't change the size of the image, just the area surrounding it. Select **Resize > Canvas Size** from the Image menu and then position the white anchor square to the right. This will add the new extra canvas to the left of the map. Select either inches or mm (whichever you prefer) and type in the new width.

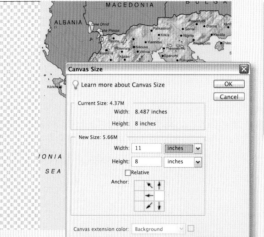

2 As we are going to add to the sea area, select the Water Mask layer and fill the area on the left with black, this fill will now be visible in the Layers palette. All the other layers also have empty space to the left, but this doesn't matter as the "new" sea will cover them.

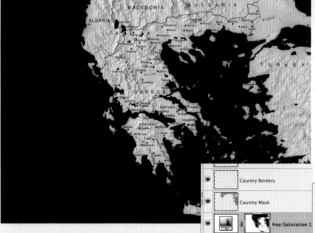

3 Ctrl/Cmd-click the Water Mask layer thumbnail to create a selection from it. Now click the Make Adjustment Layer button and select Hue/Saturation. The Country Mask layer is no longer needed, so turn it off using the Visibility Icon.

4 With the Hue/Saturation palette open check Colorize and drag the Hue slider to +216. Move the Saturation to +73 and the Lightness to +54 to create a strong blue tint for the extended sea area.

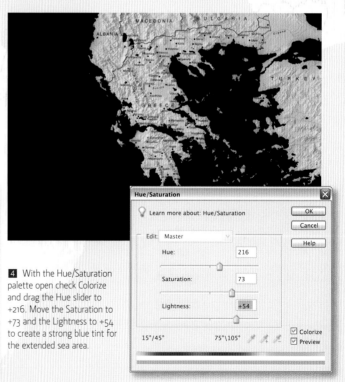

5 Now, select the Country Mask layer and create a Hue/Saturation adjustment layer, as in step 3, to make the selection. Again, check Colorize and drag the Hue slider to 43, Saturation to 16 and Lightness to -14. You now have two adjustment layers that control the entire map—except Greece itself.

6 Next select the layer Ocean/Sea/Lakes Names. Select **Adjust Color > Adjust Hue/Saturation** from the Enhance menu. As this is a text layer, we will make the change directly to the layer for the reasons discussed on page 36. With Colorize checked, drag the Lightness slider to +50. The text on this layer is now gray. With maximum Lightness, the Hue and Saturation settings now have no effect.

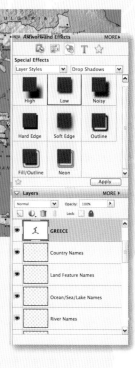

7 Create a new text layer at the top of the stack by clicking the Text tools in the active image area and type in the title GREECE. Here it is set in the font 80pt Charlemagne Bold. Click on Create Warped Text in the Options bar and select Fish. Stick with the default settings to distort the title into a fish shape.

8 The final touches are to select **Special Effects > Layer Styles > Drop Shadows > Low** from the Artwork and Effects palette to apply a drop shadow to the title, and to add a column of paragraph text to the space on the left. This is set in 13pt Arial and the opacity of this layer has been reduced to 75% so it is not too dominant.

ADDING GRAPHICS

Make Your Own Maps offers the user the flexibility to save maps in a generic format like JPEG and then add additional text and graphics in another application, or add them directly to the map using layers within Elements. You can add graphics to a map in a number of different ways and the simplest is to use Elements' Custom Shape tool to create icon style graphics such as animals or people. When you create a layer using the Custom Shape tool it creates a vector shape rather than a bitmap. A vector is just an outline path that is filled with a color, which means you can resize it without any loss of quality. If you Simplify the layer (**Layer** > **Simplify Layer**) it becomes a bitmap, and should not be subsequently enlarged.

You can also use drawing and painting tools to add borders or paths and once you've created a graphic you can clone it using the Clone Stamp tool. This is particularly useful if you want to add a lot of identical graphics without adding multiple layers. You can even import graphics from elsewhere, like those on the following spread.

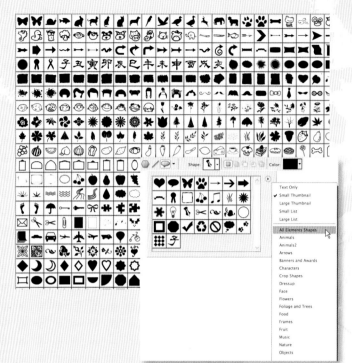

CUSTOM SHAPES
Elements has a wide variety of options when you select the Custom Shape tool. By default only a few are shown, but if you want to see all of them click the arrow on the palette and select All Elements Shapes from the flyout menu. Drag the triangle at the bottom right of the palette to enlarge it.

ADDING NOTES
1 Choose a Custom Shape—here the Thumb Tack has been selected—and click and drag the image to the size that you require on the map. Hold down the Shift key when doing so to constrain the proportions. Double-click the layer thumbnail if you want to change color. You will be able to move it to the correct position later.

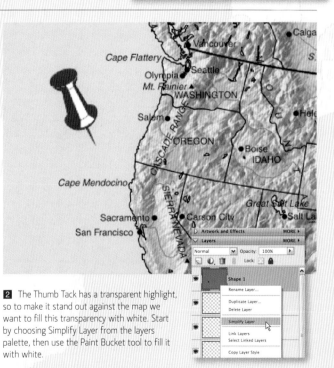

2 The Thumb Tack has a transparent highlight, so to make it stand out against the map we want to fill this transparency with white. Start by choosing Simplify Layer from the layers palette, then use the Paint Bucket tool to fill it with white.

3 Drag the Thumb Tack to a position just above Nashville. Add another Custom Shape (this time Crop Shape 13) to create a rough-edged white panel that will form the background for a text label. Position it so the Tack appears to pin it to the map. Add some text, and as a finishing touch, select a Soft Edge Drop Shadow from **Special Effects** > **Layer Styles** in the Artwork and Effects palette.

ADDING A ROUTE

1 Create a new layer above Physical: Light. Select the Brush tool from the Tools palette and in the Options bar select a 5px brush from the default Brushes menu. Further to the right in the Options bar select More Options, and change the Spacing value to 200%. The brush thumbnail has now changed to a dotted line.

2 Draw a line of dots between each location to show your route. Here, larger dots have been added to surround the ports of call (see right).

ADDING PORTS OF CALL

1 Create another new layer above Physical: Light. Select the Elliptical Marquee tool zoom into the map. Place your cursor in the center of any convenient location dot, hold down the Shift/Alt keys and drag the cursor out to create a circular selection of the desired size. Use the Paint Bucket tool to fill it with color; here a bright red.

2 Hit Ctrl/Cmd+D to remove the selection and then choose the Clone Stamp tool from the Tools Palette. In the Options Bar select one of the harder edge brushes at the top of the Default Brushes menu and increase the size so that it is about three or four times the size of the red dot, and place the cursor above it.

3 To clone the dot, select the Clone tool from the Toolbar and choose a brush slightly larger than the dot. Place the cursor over your first red dot, hold down the Alt/Opt key and click to select the dot as your "source." Move the cursor to where you want another dot and click again to add a cloned dot. Repeat this process to create each of your "ports of call."

37

ADDING GRAPHICS

Using the Brush tool with extra spacing gives you the option of creating a dotted or broken line. On the previous spread it was a freehand line, but here it is constrained to straight lines—ideal for the creation of a border. Always remember to select the foreground color first, as once you have used a brush, the color can only be changed retrospectively by using Hue/Saturation. When you rescale map layers it is best to apply the change to all layers, even those you don't intend to use, because if you change your mind later and try to rescale an individual layer, you will have difficulty aligning it with the others. Once you have made the change, simply turn off the unwanted layers. You can also add graphics created outside Elements by copy/pasting them into new layers, and even use selections made from map layers to crop them perfectly.

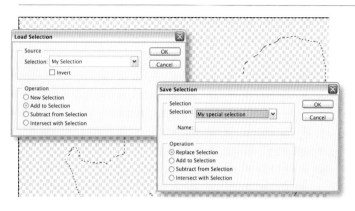

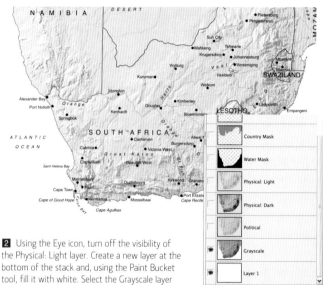

ADDING A NATIONAL FLAG

1 Select the Water Mask layer and Ctrl/Cmd-click the layer thumbnail to make a selection. Go to the Select menu, choose Save Selection and give it a name like "My special selection." Do the same for the Country Mask layer to make another selection. Return to the Select menu and choose Load Selection. Be sure to check Add to Selection. The result is a selection around South Africa. Return to the Select menu and choose Save Selection, this time making sure that Replace Selection is checked. Save the map and you will be able to load this selection again in the future.

2 Using the Eye icon, turn off the visibility of the Physical: Light layer. Create a new layer at the bottom of the stack and, using the Paint Bucket tool, fill it with white. Select the Grayscale layer above and reduce its opacity to 50%.

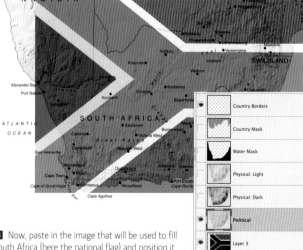

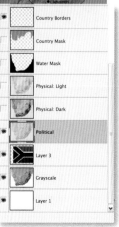

3 Now, paste in the image that will be used to fill South Africa (here the national flag) and position it immediately above the Grayscale layer. To rescale and position it correctly, turn on the visibility of the Political layer and reduce its opacity to about 60% so you can see the flag beneath it.

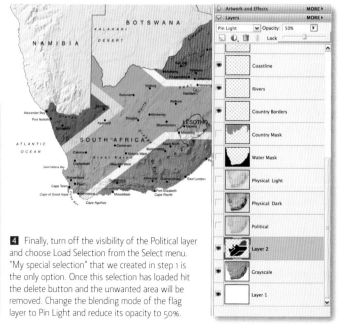

4 Finally, turn off the visibility of the Political layer and choose Load Selection from the Select menu. "My special selection" that we created in step 1 is the only option. Once this selection has loaded hit the delete button and the unwanted area will be removed. Change the blending mode of the flag layer to Pin Light and reduce its opacity to 50%.

ADDING A CUSTOM BORDER

1 Create a new layer at the top of the stack and select the Brush tool from the toolbar. In the Options bar, select a 24px brush from the Square Brushes menu. Further to the right in the Options bar select More Options, and change the Spacing value to 200%. The brush thumbnail has now changed to a broken line.

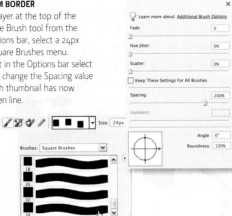

2 Turn off all the map layers using the visibility icon in the Layers palette, apart from your new layer. With the new layer selected, zoom into the top left of the map and position the cursor. Click and drag to the right. The active image area will scroll as you move the cursor, so don't stop until you get to the end. Repeat this process on the other three sides.

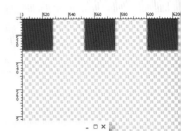

3 Next, select all the map layers and click the Link button in the Layers palette. Turn on the visibility of the layers you plan to use. Make sure that the new border layer is not linked or selected. Now, using the Move tool and with the Shift and Alt/Opt keys pressed, drag any corner of the map in towards the center and click the Commit Arrow.

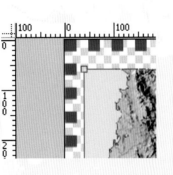

39

MATCHING THE CANVAS SIZE TO THE BRUSH REPEAT

When you use a brush to draw a repeat, it is helpful if the Canvas size is divisible by the size of the brush you have chosen. That way you do not end up short of the perimeter, or with only half the brush stroke visible. In the Canvas Size palette you will need to change from ins or mm to pixels as your unit. Here the Canvas has been changed by a few pixels so that it is now 1272 x 1224px to reflect the 12px brush size.

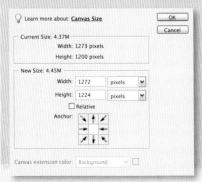

4 Select the Physical: Dark layer and Ctrl/Cmd-click to create a selection from it. Making sure you have one of the Selection tools selected in the toolbar, move the selection down using the arrow keys. Use the Eyedropper tool to sample the blue sea and paint in the extra sea. Remember to change back to the default brush before you paint.

ADDING GRAPHIC EFFECTS

In addition to creating extra graphics for a map, exciting graphic effects can be applied to the existing map's layers. Once again, adjustment layers provide the means, and these are particularly useful when changing the colors of multiple layers, where you'll invariably need to tweak an adjacent color. The adjustment layer will apply to the entire image unless a selection has first been made, so always remember to Ctrl/Cmd-click on the layer thumbnail to make a perfect selection. Photoshop Elements' Artwork and Effects palette includes many great effects, but some do not work well on black or monochrome layers, while others require prior selection of foreground and background colors. Layer Styles—in particular Drop Shadows—are very useful for highlighting a specific area and giving the map a lift. In Elements 5, Drop Shadows are fully editable, so you can change the lighting angle, size, distance, and opacity of the shadow, and apply extra features like bevels, glows, and strokes. In Elements 4 the controls are generally more limited.

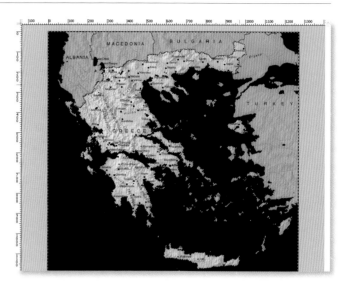

1 With the Water Mask layer selected, Ctrl/Cmd-click the layer thumbnail to make a selection. From the Select menu choose Save Selection and give it a name like "My special selection." Repeat the process for the Country Mask layer to create another selection. Choose Load Selection from the Select menu and check Add to Selection. This creates a selection around Greece. Now, from the Select menu choose Save Selection, this time with Replace Selection checked. Don't forget to Save before proceeding, in order to be able to use this selection again in the future.

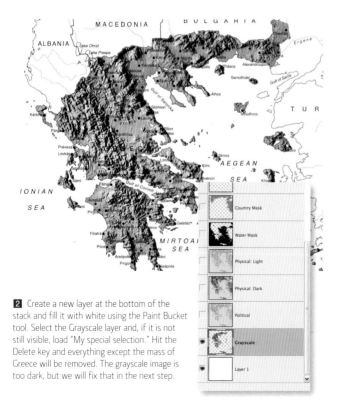

2 Create a new layer at the bottom of the stack and fill it with white using the Paint Bucket tool. Select the Grayscale layer and, if it is not still visible, load "My special selection." Hit the Delete key and everything except the mass of Greece will be removed. The grayscale image is too dark, but we will fix that in the next step.

3 With the Grayscale layer still selected, Ctrl/Cmd-click the layer thumbnail to make a selection. Use the Create Adjustment Layer button on the Layers palette to add a Hue/Saturation adjustment layer. Ensure Colorize is checked and drag the Hue slider to 58, Saturation to 77, and Lightness to +34. The grayscale image is now a green-yellow.

4 Select the Water Mask layer and repeat step 3, but this time drag the Hue slider to 178, Saturation to 65, and Lightness to +48. The Water Mask image is now a blue-green and the adjacent countries are the only remaining uncolored areas.

If you don't like the white land mass for the adjacent countries then create a selection from the Country Mask layer and apply a color to it, as described in steps 2 and 3. Turn off the Coastline and Country Borders layers using the visibility icon.

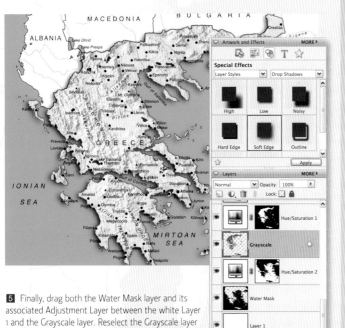

5 Finally, drag both the Water Mask layer and its associated Adjustment Layer between the white Layer 1 and the Grayscale layer. Reselect the Grayscale layer and from the Artwork and Effects palette select Soft Edge from the **Layer Styles > Drop Shadows** options.

If you turn off the Grayscale layer, the Adjustment Layer above it will still define the shape, but you will have to change the Hue/Saturation settings. Here the Lightness has been dragged back to -46, the Hue is 58, and the Saturation 77. The result is a flat color, but if you want to retain the drop shadow you can apply it to the Adjustment Layer.

ADDING GRAPHIC EFFECTS

With the exception of Photoshop itself, no application has as many special effects as Elements, so it is best to apply them to your maps before saving them in a generic format like JPEG. You can apply Elements effects and styles to radically alter the look of a map—in fact you can create an entirely new texture and color by using selections created from the Water Mask and Country Mask layers to replace the physical layers altogether. Using a technique like this is great fun, although as you sacrifice the topographical detail for the sake of a graphic effect use this technique sparingly, and only when geographical integrity is not paramount. In the examples here, effects have been applied exclusively to the land mass or sea areas. Apart from changing the text color it is best to avoid applying graphic effects and styles to the map text, as it is just too small to benefit from these techniques.

1 Add a new layer (Layer 1) at the bottom of the stack and fill it with white using the Paint Bucket tool. Ctrl/Cmd-click the Water Mask layer thumbnail to create a selection from it, and choose Inverse from the Select menu. Create a new layer (Layer 2) and fill with a mid gray. Select the Water Mask layer again and, using Hue/Saturation from the **Enhance > Adjust Color** menu, use the Lightness slider to reduce the black areas to mid-gray.

2 Reselect Layer 2 and, from the Artwork and Effects palette, select Wow Plastic Orange from the **Layer Styles > Special Effects** options. This transforms the land mass, giving it a toffee-colored shine. Here the default values have been used, although they can be fully edited in Elements 5.

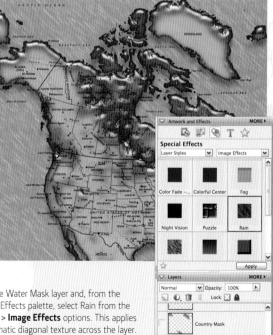

3 Select the Water Mask layer and, from the Artwork and Effects palette, select Rain from the **Layer Styles > Image Effects** options. This applies a monochromatic diagonal texture across the layer.

4 With the Water Mask layer still selected there are two ways of adding color. One is to use Hue/Saturation, and the other—that we have used here—comes from the Artwork and Effects palette. Here we used Blue Tone from the **Layer Styles > Photographic Effects** options.

1 In Elements 5 the Wow Plastic Orange layer style applied to Layer 2 is fully editable. Surprisingly, when you uncheck all the controls the toffee color remains. Here we have retained only a drop shadow, altering the color and size a little, and changing the angle to 120˚. The Water Mask layer has also been turned off using the visibility icon.

2 With Layer 2 still selected, change the blending mode to Overlay. Now, select the Grayscale layer and reduce the layer opacity to 40%. The result is a blend of the Grayscale layer relief and the Wow Plastic Orange layer style.

5 In this final version, the Coastline layer visibility has been turned off.

43

MONTAGING MAPS WITH PHOTOGRAPHS

When you use *Make Your Own Maps* in a project you will probably want to add photographs as well as graphics and text. As Elements creates a new layer for each item that is pasted in, it's possible to blend this new material with the existing map layers to create some stunning looking documents. Before you proceed it may be necessary to add some extra background to a map to accommodate the new images. Photos can be added as conventional squared-up images, or integrated into a map in a more decorative way. You can also use a detail of the map, although this may mean the new crop cuts through the middle of some map names. There are two solutions to this— use the Eraser tool to remove test at the edges before copying the detail, or feather the edges to soften the detail.

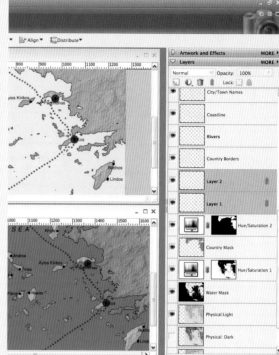

> ### TIP
>
> **ADDING EXTRA BACKGROUND**
> Select **Resize** > **Canvas Size** from the Image menu. Position the white anchor square to determine where the extra background will appear. Select either inches or mm, and type in the new width. The additional image area is shown as gray checkerboard.

1 The starting point for this project is the extended map from page 34, but without the new text layers. We have then added the two route layers from the map on page 37. To do this, have both maps open, and drag the layers from one map to the other. Move them into position below the Country Borders layer and, while they are both still selected, click the Link button in the Layers palette.

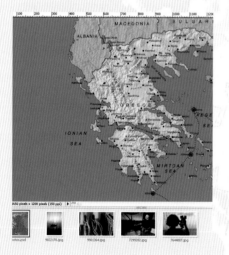

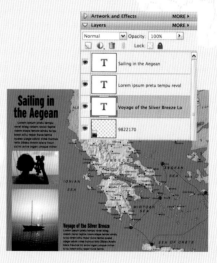

2 Open the photos that you plan to use so they appear in the Photo Bin. When you are working on the map you can collapse the Photo Bin by clicking on the handle. Elements always fits the photos into the active image area, but this doesn't reflect their actual size, which is shown as both a percentage scaling, and resolution (ppi). The maps are all 150 ppi, while photos from your digital camera are likely to be 72ppi.

3 Having selected the top layer, drag an image out of the Photo Bin and onto the map. Rescale the photo to a convenient size and click the Commit Arrow. To drag is to make a copy of that image; the image in the bin will stay intact. Repeat the process with a second image and position them, leaving some space for a title at the top.

4 Select the Horizontal Type tool, click on the map to create a new layer at the top of the stack and add your title text. Add another two text layers, using a smaller font for the additional information.

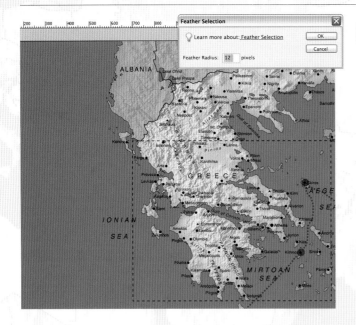

1 Use the Rectangular Marquee tool to make a selection in the area of the map containing the route. From the Select menu, choose Feather and accept the default 12px radius. Feathering creates a soft edge to the selection, while the radius sets the number of pixels either side of the edge of the selection that are affected.

2 From the Edit menu select Copy Merged. Then, choose New Blank File from the File menu and set the dimensions to 11 x 8in (280 x 203mm) at a resolution of 150ppi. Select Paste from the Edit menu and the map detail—with a soft edge—will appear in the center of the image. Drag it towards top right.

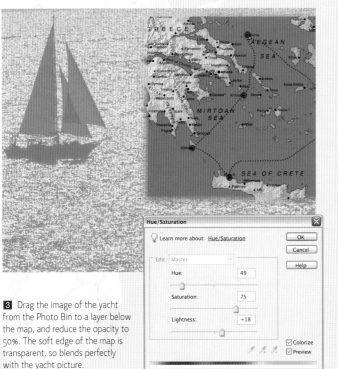

Sailing in the Aegean

Lorem ipsum pretu tempu revol bileg rokam revoc tephe rosve etepe tenov sindu turqu brevt elliu repar tiuve tamia queso uta

3 Drag the image of the yacht from the Photo Bin to a layer below the map, and reduce the opacity to 50%. The soft edge of the map is transparent, so blends perfectly with the yacht picture.

4 With the yacht layer selected, choose Hue/Saturation from the **Image > Adjustments** menu. Ensure Colorize is checked and drag the Hue slider to the left until the yacht layer is yellow. Adjust the Saturation and Lightness until the desired color is achieved. The finishing touch is to create text layers for the heading and text.

MONTAGING MAPS WITH PHOTOGRAPHS

The power and versatility of Elements means the only limiting factor is your imagination! Simply adding photos to a project may not be enough—you may want replace an entire map feature with a photo. One of the problems that may arise with this approach is the sacrifice of text legibility in the pursuit of a striking design. There are various ways of avoiding this, such as not using an image that is too busy or that contains too much contrast. If this is the case, lighten the image or use a filter to blur it. One of the useful by-products of using a blurred image is that it is possible to use a

low resolution photo, or even enlarge it, as the blur will disguise its defects. Color invariably adds to complexity, so if all else fails use Hue/Saturation with Colorize checked to convert an image. This makes good text legibility more likely, and can provide a more dramatic visual effect. Other tools that Elements provides—like Brightness/Contrast and Adjust Color Curves—can also be used to flatten or desaturate the images.

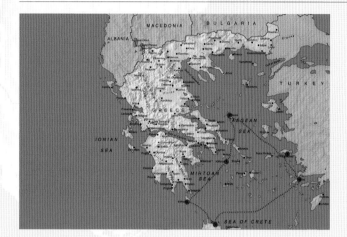

1 Again the starting point for this project is the extended map on page 34, but without the new text layers. We have also added the route layers from the map on page 37, using the "drag and drop" method described on the previous pages to drag the layers from one image to another. Position the route layers below the Country Borders layer and click the Link button in the Layers palette to lock them together.

2 With the Physical: Light layer selected, choose the "My special selection" we created on page 38 from the **Select > Load Selection** menu and hit the Delete key. Turn off the visibility for the Country Mask and Water Mask layers and their associated adjustment layers.

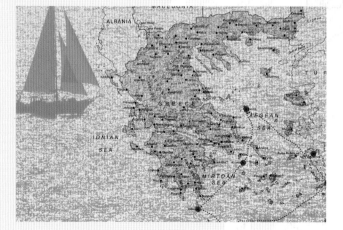

3 Drag the boat image from the Photo Bin onto the map below the Physical: Light layer. Don't worry if the result looks a mess! The next step is to reduce the opacity of the yacht layer to 50%. Zoom out in order to scale and position the boat in relation to the map.

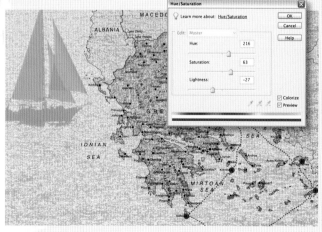

4 With the yacht layer still selected create a Hue/Saturation adjustment layer. With Colorize checked, drag the Hue slider to 216, the Saturation to 63, and the Lightness to -27. The boat image is now a mid-blue.

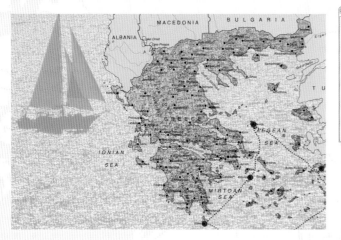

5 Select the Country Mask layer and increase the layer opacity to 100%. Select the Country Mask Hue/Saturation adjustment layer, and, with Colorize checked, drag the Hue slider to 115, Saturation to 21, and Lightness to +30. This changes the adjacent countries to pale green.

6 Select the Physical: Light layer and, from the Artwork and Effects palette, select Soft Edge from the **Layer Styles > Drop Shadows** options. The default options need to be changed because of the small island shapes, so edit the Lighting Angle to 90˚, the Drop Shadow size to 10px, Distance to 5px and Opacity to 50%.

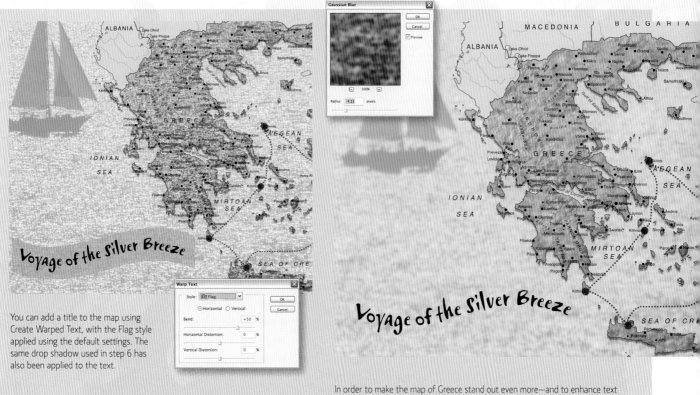

You can add a title to the map using Create Warped Text, with the Flag style applied using the default settings. The same drop shadow used in step 6 has also been applied to the text.

In order to make the map of Greece stand out even more—and to enhance text legibility—the yacht layer has been blurred. With the yacht layer selected from the Artwork and Effects palette, select Gaussian Blur from the **Special Effects > Filters** options and drag the slider to 4px.

PUTTING IT ALL TOGETHER

This project brings together many of the techniques described previously in this chapter; adding photos, adding text, creating graphics, using brushes, applying special effects, as well as extending map layers. Fortunately, even quite complex projects consist of a series of simple steps; making changes to existing layers and adding new ones. If you make a mistake, Undo is only a click away. Elements' user-friendly interface has been designed to help with every task and opening and closing both the Photo and Palette Bins instantly provides extra workspace. Special effects like Bevels and Drop

Shadows are easily applied, and give images a three-dimensional effect at the click of a button. Even if your drawing skills are zero, using the right tools makes tasks simple—like creating the string used on this project—and you can always try things several times until you're satisfied with the result.

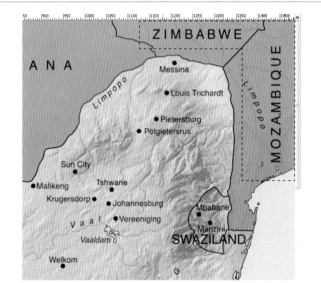

1 Using the Rectangular Marquee tool, make a selection around the names in the top right corner of the map. Select the Country Names layer and press Delete to remove them. Now, select the Oceans/Seas/ Lakes Names layer and do the same to remove the river names. Finally, make selections around the text "ATLANTIC OCEAN" and "INDIAN OCEAN" and move them to new locations closer to the coastline.

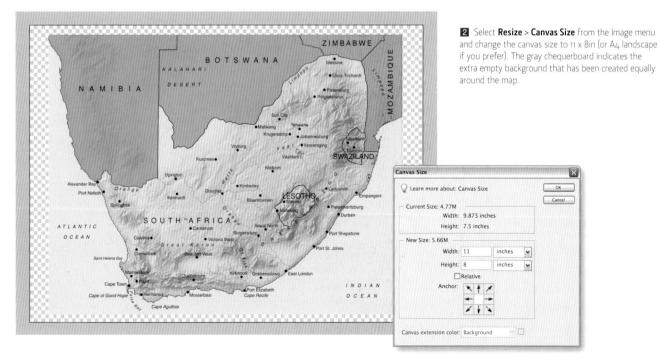

2 Select **Resize** > **Canvas Size** from the Image menu and change the canvas size to 11 x 8in (or A4 landscape if you prefer). The gray chequerboard indicates the extra empty background that has been created equally around the map.

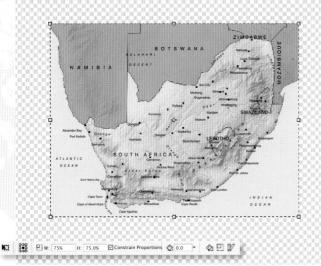

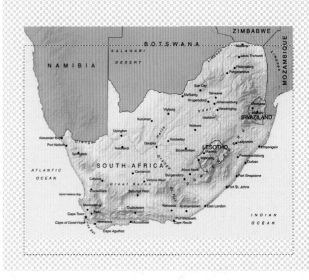

3 Remove any remaining selections and select all the layers in the Layers palette. Click the Link Layers button. Next, select any of the eight handles of the Bounding box to make the Transform settings appear in the Options bar. With Constrain Proportions checked, change either Width or Height to 75%, and click the Commit tick.

4 With only the Physical: Light layer selected (but all layers still linked), Ctrl/Cmd-click the layer thumbnail to make a selection. With one of the Selection tools selected in the Toolbar use the Arrow Keys to move the selection down.

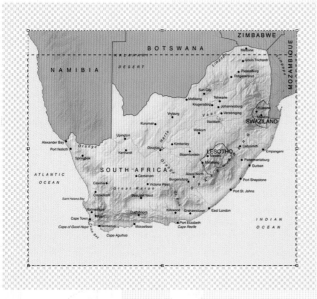

5 With the Physical: Light layer still selected, use the Eyedropper tool to sample the blue sea color. Using either the Paint Bucket tool or a large brush and the Paint Brush tool, add sea to the bottom of the map. The selection will prevent you from going over the bottom edge or sides.

6 Click on the small black and white icon at the base of the Toolbar to restore the default colors. Select the layer below Physical: Light and choose the Custom Shape tool from the toolbar. From the Options bar select Suitcase and, starting from bottom left or right, drag the cursor until the case encloses the map. The suitcase shape is filled with black.

Putting it all together

7 Select the Country Mask layer and increase the layer opacity to 100%. Use the Eyedropper tool to sample the gray, and then select a brush of about 50px before roughly painting over the handle area.

8 Reselect the suitcase Shape 1 layer and Ctrl/Cmd-click the layer thumbnail to make a selection. From the Select menu choose Inverse and reselect the Country Mask layer. Hit the delete key to remove the unwanted background from this layer. Repeat the process with the Physical: Light, Coastline, Rivers and Country Borders layers.

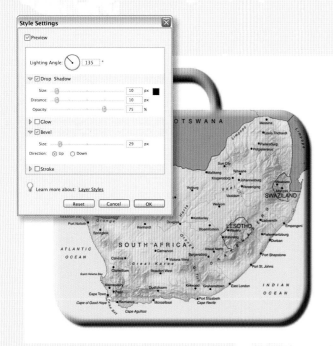

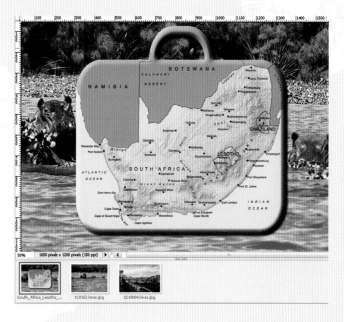

9 Check that all the layers that were linked in step 3 are still linked and then click the More button in the Layers palette. Select Merge Linked from the options so all the linked layers are merged into a single layer. From the Artwork and Effects palette select Simple Inner from the **Layer Styles > Bevels** options. Change the Lighting Angle to 135˚ and Bevel Size to 29px. Elements 5 enables you to select a Drop Shadow as well, so check this box.

10 Open some suitable South African background images so they appear in the Photo Bin. Drag the one you want to use into the active image area, below the suitcase layer. Scale and position it to fill the canvas.

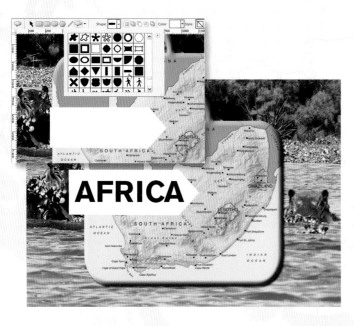

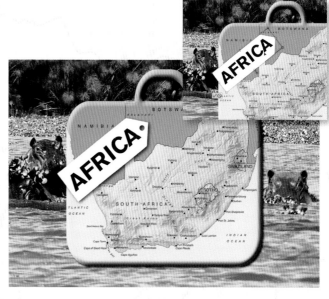

11 To add the label, select the Custom Shape tool from the toolbar. From the Options bar, select Sign 7 and drag the cursor until a label shape has been formed. Select the Horizontal Type tool and create a new layer with the title text at the top of the layer stack. Select both layers and select Merge Visible from the layers palette.

12 Use the bounding box handles to rotate and rescale the label and then, with the Elliptical Marquee tool, draw a circle and hit the delete key to punch a "hole" in it. From the Artwork and Effects palette, select Soft Edge from the **Special Effects > Layer Styles > Drop Shadows** palette.

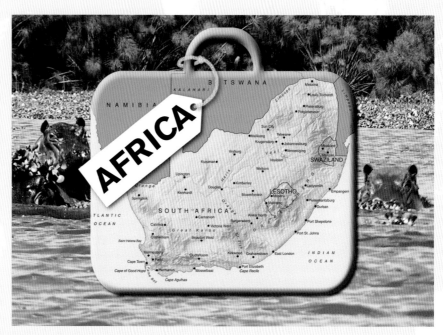

13 Create a new layer at the top of the stack and with the Brush tool selected, choose Pastel Rough Texture from the Dry Media Brushes. The size should be about 15 px. With a beige foreground color selected, draw a piece of string connecting the label with the handle.

14 Zoom in to the string and use the Freehand Lasso tool to select the area of string to be removed, so it appears to go round the back of the handle. Hit the Delete key to remove it and apply the same drop shadow used on the label.

PRINTING

When you print an image there are two variable factors: the application you are printing from and the printer you are printing to. Applications vary in the options they offer, so printing a map in Elements will be very different from printing a document from MS Word. Printers differ to. When you install a printer, the software that runs it—known as the driver—will make all the features of that particular model available to each application on your computer. This makes generalizations about printing somewhat difficult, but there are key features that apply to all, and they are described on this page. The Windows PC and Mac print palettes are slightly different and the version of the operating system you're using will also affect the look. These screen grabs are from Windows Vista. Always use the best quality paper and best print quality settings when printing the maps. This is particularly important when the map text is small.

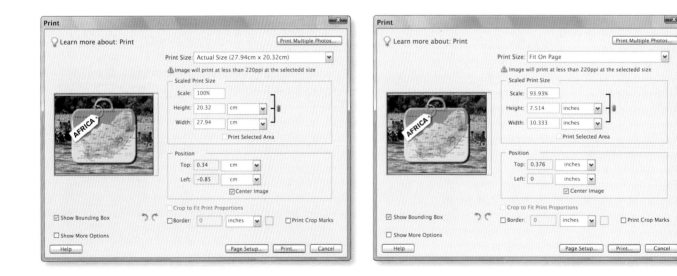

1 When printing from Elements, the Print Preview palette displays a yellow triangle alert icon, with a message that the print will be at less than 220ppi. You can safely ignore this as all the maps have been created at 150dpi, which is fine for printing actual size on any desktop printer. Most maps fit within the Letter format of 8 x 11in (203 x 280mm) and if you have an edge-to-edge printer you will be able to print without reduction. By default, Elements assumes that you will be printing Actual Size.

2 If your printer requires a margin around the edge then choose the Fit on Page option. Although it will be grayed out, you can see the reduction that will be applied; here it's 93.93%. This small reduction will not affect the quality or legibility of a map.

Print dialog (top left)

Print

Learn more about: Print

Print Multiple Photos...

Print Size: Fit On Page

⚠ Image will print at less than 220ppi at the selectedd size

Scaled Print Size

Scale: 93.93%

Height: 7.514 inches

Width: 10.333 inches

☐ Print Selected Area

Position

Top: 0.376 inches

Left: 0 inches

☑ Center Image

☐ Crop to Fit Print Proportions

☑ Show Bounding Box   ☐ Border: 0 inches   ☐ Print Crop Marks

☐ Show More Options

Help   Page Setup...   Print...   Cancel

---

3 Many people use the installed default settings when printing, and of course they vary from printer to printer. One thing you do have to specify is the orientation and you will find this in Page Setup. The thumbnail image on the Print Preview palette will reflect this choice, so if you haven't already done so, use the Page Setup button to select either Portrait or Landscape.

Print dialog (bottom left)

Print

Printer

Name: \\GRAHAM\Epson Stylus COLOR 1520 ▼   Properties...

Status: Ready
Type: Epson Stylus COLOR 1520 ESC/P2
Where: LPT1:
Comment: ☐ Print to file

Print range
◉ All
○ Pages from: ___ to: ___
○ Selection

Copies
Number of copies: 1

1 1 2 2 3 3   ☐ Collate

OK   Cancel

---

4 If you are unsure of your printer's settings, click the Properties button. Normally you will be able to select the media type, and that should match the grade of paper currently in your printer. There will also be print quality settings and they too should match the paper. There is little point using the highest quality setting if you aren't using a high quality paper as you will just be wasting ink.

PRINT SETTINGS

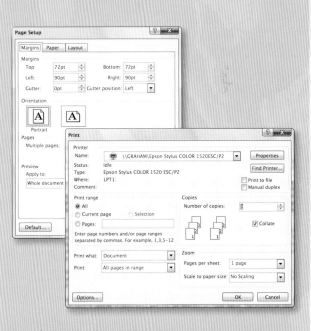

Epson Stylus COLOR 1520ESC/P2 on GRAHAM Printing Preferences

Layout | Paper/Quality | Utilities

Tray Selection
Paper Source: Automatically Select
Media: Photo Quality Glossy Paper

Quality Settings
◉ Best   ○ Normal   ○ Draft

Color
○ Black & White

Epson Stylus COLOR 1520ESC/P2 Advanced Options

Epson Stylus COLOR1520ESC/P2 Advanced Document

Paper/Output
  Paper Size: Letter
  Copy Count: 1 Copy
Graphic
  Print Quality Super Fine
  Image Color Super Fine
    ICM Meth Fine ... by Host System
    ICOM Intent: Pictures
Document Options
  Advanced Printing Features: Enabled
  Pages per Sheet Layout: Right then Down
Printer Features
  Printable Area: Maximum
  Override With Presets: Automatic (Quality
  Hight Speed: Off
  Microweave: On

OK   Cancel

When you select Printing Preferences, the default is usually a basic configuration, with a button showing Advanced options. Here, checking the "Best" button in the Quality Settings gives a further choice of Fine and Super Fine in the Advanced options.

Page Setup

Margins | Paper | Layout

Margins
Top: 72pt   Bottom: 72pt
Left: 90pt   Right: 90pt
Gutter: 0pt Gutter position: Left

Orientation
Portrait

Pages
Multiple pages:

Preview
Apply to:
Whole document

Default...

Print

Printer
Name: \\GRAHAM\Epson Stylus COLOR 1520ESC/P2 ▼   Properties
Status: Idle   Find Printer...
Type: Epson Stylus COLOR 1520 ESC/P2
Where: LPT1:   ☐ Print to file
Comment: ☐ Manual duplex

Print range
◉ All
○ Current page   ○ Selection
○ Pages: ___
Enter page numbers and/or page ranges
separated by commas. For example, 1,3,5–12

Copies
Number of copies: 1
☑ Collate

Print what: Document
Print: All pages in range

Zoom
Pages per sheet: 1 page
Scale to paper size: No Scaling

Options...   OK   Cancel

Microsoft Word's Page Setup and Print palettes are very different from Photoshop Elements', even though they're both printing to the same printer.

Map list

54

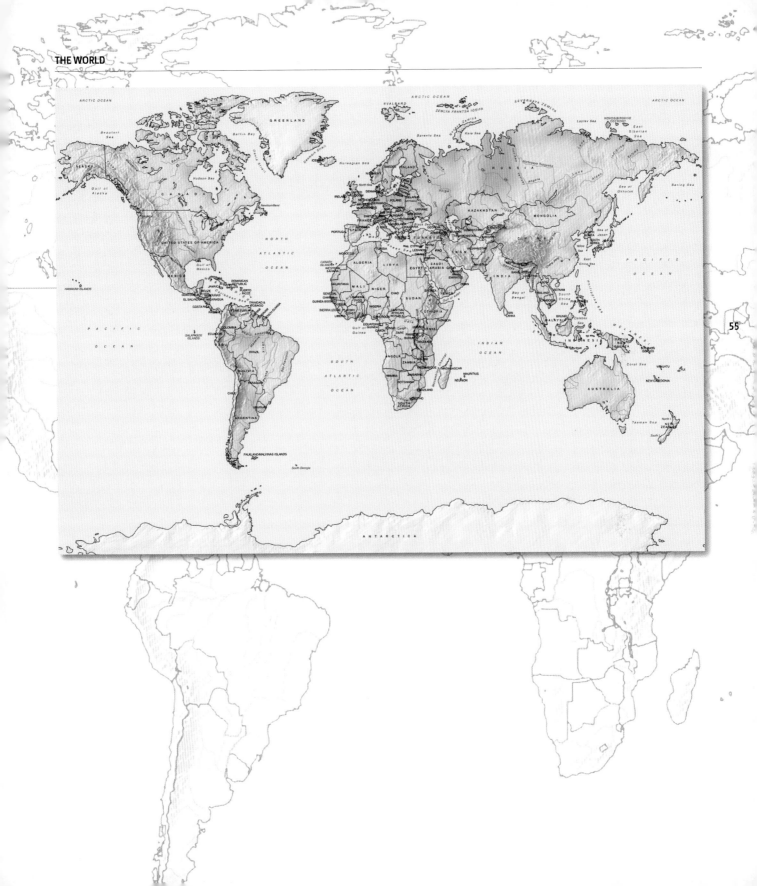

NORTH AMERICA

SOUTH AMERICA

CARIBBEAN +CENTRAL AMERICA

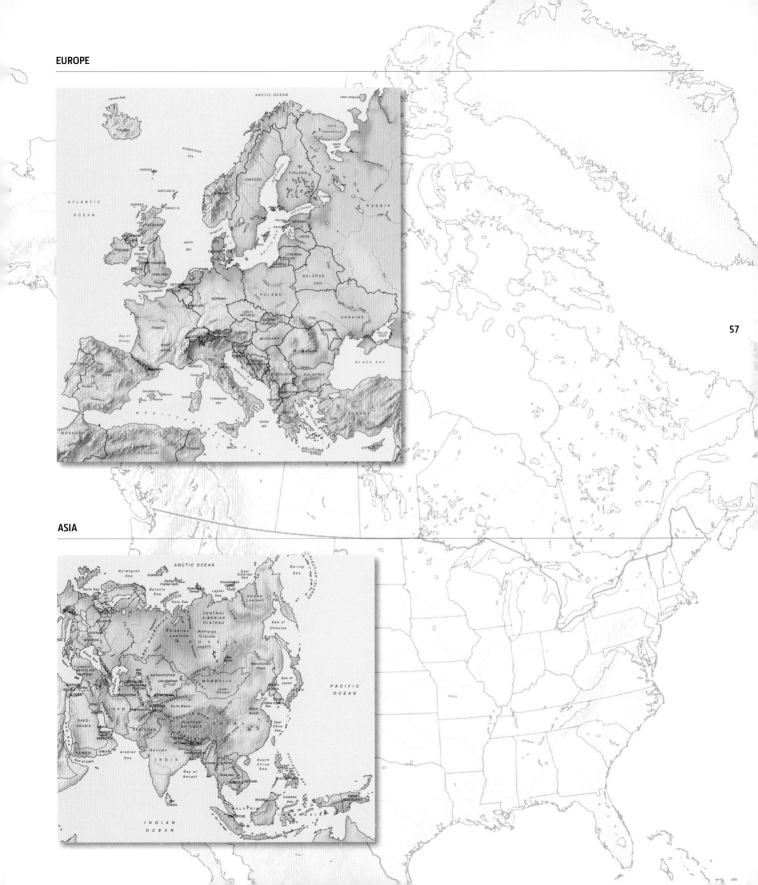

EUROPE

ASIA

57

AFRICA

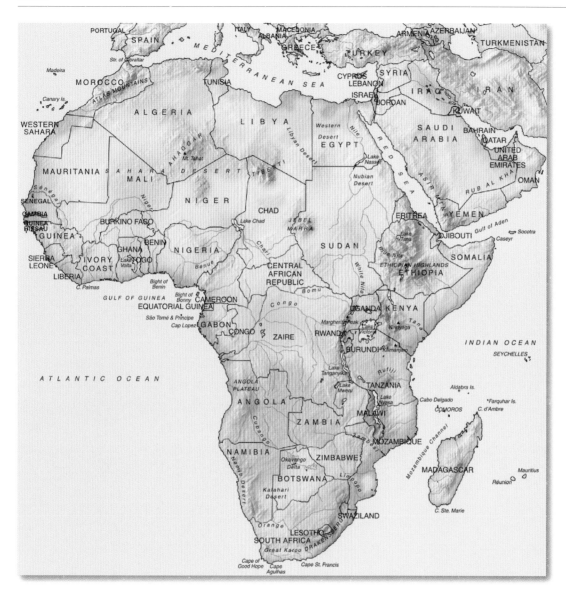

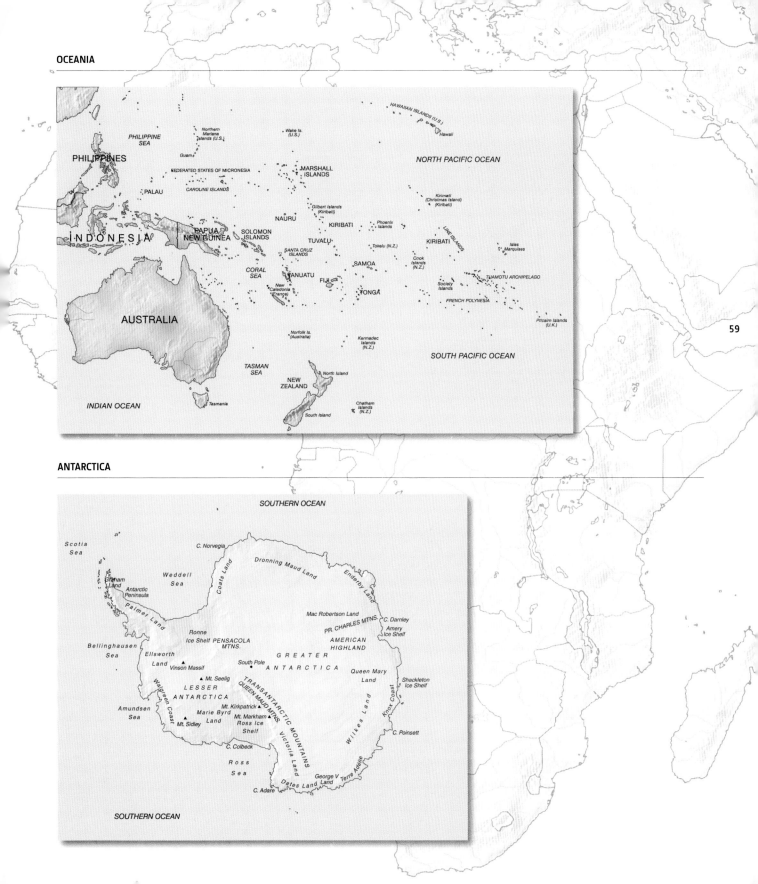

OCEANIA

PHILIPPINE
SEA

PHILIPPINES

Northern
Mariana
Islands (U.S.)

Wake Is.
(U.S.)

HAWAIIAN ISLANDS (U.S.)

Hawaii

Guam

FEDERATED STATES OF MICRONESIA

NORTH PACIFIC OCEAN

PALAU

CAROLINE ISLANDS

MARSHALL
ISLANDS

Kiritati
(Christmas Island)
(Kiribati)

NAURU

Gilbert Islands
(Kiribati)

KIRIBATI

Phoenix
Islands

LINE ISLANDS

Isles
Marquises

INDONESIA

PAPUA
NEW GUINEA

SOLOMON
ISLANDS

TUVALU

Tokelau (N.Z.)

KIRIBATI

SANTA CRUZ
ISLANDS

SAMOA

Cook
Islands
(N.Z.)

TUAMOTU ARCHIPELAGO

CORAL
SEA

VANUATU

FIJI

New
Caledonia
(France)

TONGA

Society
Islands

FRENCH POLYNESIA

AUSTRALIA

Pitcairn Islands
(U.K.)

Norfolk Is.
(Australia)

Karmadec
Islands
(N.Z.)

SOUTH PACIFIC OCEAN

TASMAN
SEA

North Island

NEW
ZEALAND

Chatham
Islands
(N.Z.)

INDIAN OCEAN

Tasmania

South Island

59

SOUTHERN OCEAN

Scotia
Sea

C. Norvegia

Dronning Maud Land

Coats Land

Enderby Land

Weddell
Sea

Graham
Land

Antarctic
Peninsula

Palmer Land

Mac Robertson Land

PR. CHARLES MTNS.

C. Darnley

Amery
Ice Shelf

Ronne
Ice Shelf

PENSACOLA
MTNS.

AMERICAN
HIGHLAND

Bellinghausen
Sea

Ellsworth
Land

Vinson Massif

GREATER

ANTARCTICA

South Pole

Queen Mary
Land

Shackleton
Ice Shelf

Mt. Seelig

LESSER

Mt. Kirkpatrick

Knox Coast

Amundsen
Sea

Walgreen Coast

ANTARCTICA

Marie Byrd
Land

Mt. Markham

Wilkes Land

C. Poinsett

Mt. Sidley

Ross Ice
Shelf

Victoria Land

TRANSANTARCTIC MOUNTAINS
QUEEN MAUD MTNS.

C. Colbeck

Ross
Sea

Oates Land

George V
Land

Terre Adélie

C. Adare

SOUTHERN OCEAN

ARCTIC

ATLANTIC OCEAN

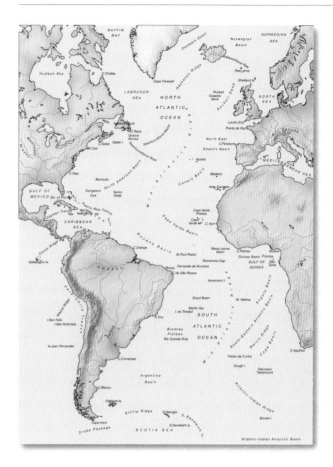

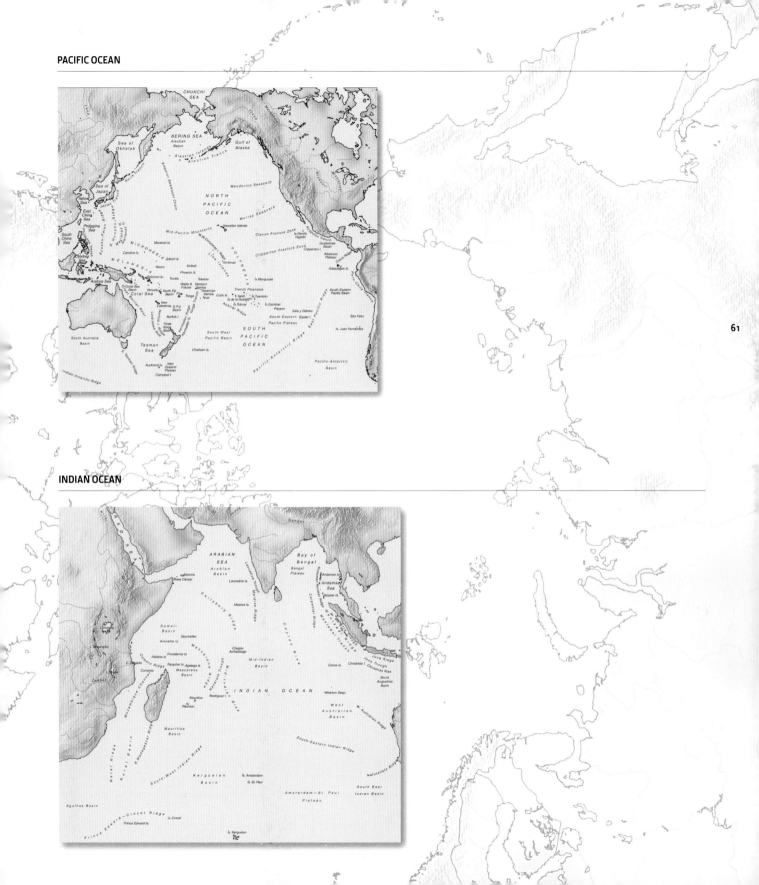

CANADA

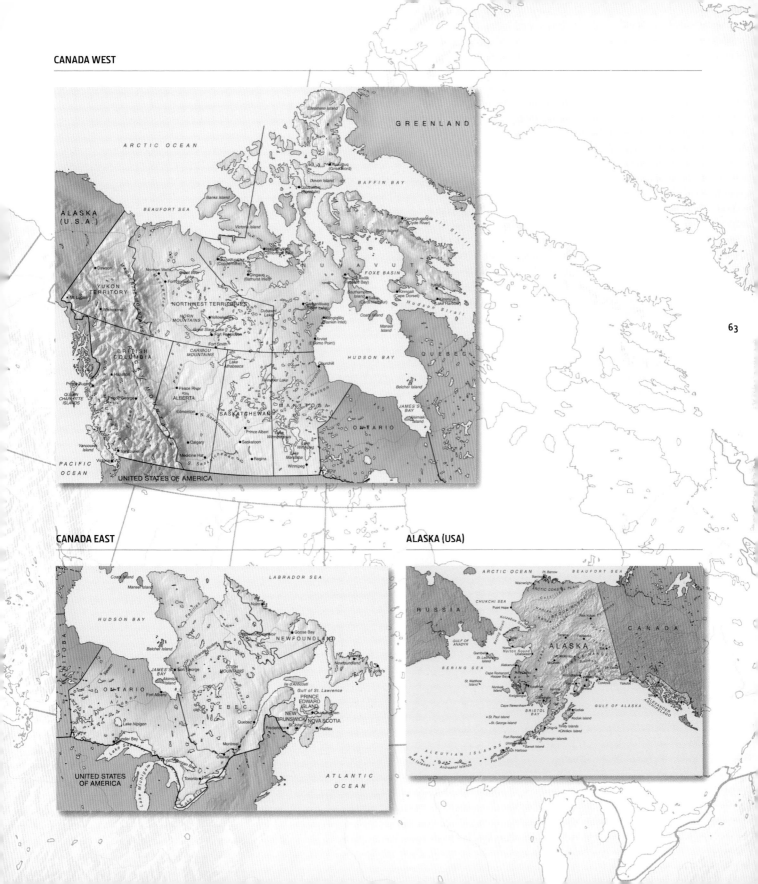

CANADA WEST

ARCTIC OCEAN

GREENLAND

Ellesmere Island

Devon Island

BAFFIN BAY

Banks Island

BEAUFORT SEA

ALASKA
(U.S.A.)

Victoria Island

Kangiqtugaapik
(Clyde River)

Baffin Island

Dawson

Norman Wells

Great Bear
Lake

Fort Norman

YUKON
Territory

Mt. Logan

Whitehorse

NORTHWEST TERRITORIES

Ikaluktutiak
(Cambridge Bay)

Qingauq
Bathurst Inlet

Igloolik
Cape Dorset

HORN
MOUNTAINS

Yellowknife

Great Slave Lake

Fort Resolution

Dubawnt
Lake

N U N A V U T

FOXE BASIN

Naujaat Aivilik
(Repulse Bay)

Iqaluit

BRITISH
COLUMBIA

CARIBOU
MOUNTAINS

Fort Smith

Lake
Athabasca

Kangiqliniq
(Rankin Inlet)

Southampton
Island

Salliq
(Coral Harbour)

Kinngait
(Cape Dorset)

Kimmirut
(Lake Harbour)

Arviat
(Eskimo Point)

Coats Island

Mansel
Island

Hudson Strait

QUEBEC

Hazelton

Peace River

Prince Rupert

Prince George

ALBERTA

Churchill

Reindeer Lake

HUDSON BAY

Belcher Island

QUEEN
CHARLOTTE
ISLANDS

Edmonton

N. Saskatchewan

SASKATCHEWAN

MANITOBA

O N T A R I O

JAMES
BAY

Akimiski
Island

Vancouver
Island

Prince Albert

Saskatoon

Calgary

Medicine Hat

Lake
Winnipeg

Regina

Lake
Manitoba

S. Saskatchewan

Winnipeg

Vancouver

Victoria

PACIFIC
OCEAN

UNITED STATES OF AMERICA

63

CANADA EAST

LABRADOR SEA

Coats Island

Mansel Island

HUDSON BAY

Nain

Belcher Island

Goose Bay

Fables

OTISH
MOUNTAINS

MANITOBA

NEWFOUNDLAND

JAMES
BAY

Fort George

Akimiski
Island

O N T A R I O

Fort Albany

La Grande Rivière

Newfoundland

St. John's

Île d'Anticosti

Q U E B E C

Lake Nipigon

Gulf of St. Lawrence

PRINCE
EDWARD
ISLAND

NEW
BRUNSWICK

NOVA SCOTIA

Thunder Bay

Quebec

Fredericton

St. John

Halifax

Montreal

Lake Superior

UNITED STATES
OF AMERICA

Georgian Bay

Ottawa

ATLANTIC
OCEAN

Lake Michigan

Toronto

Lake Huron

ALASKA (USA)

ARCTIC OCEAN

BEAUFORT SEA

Pt. Barrow

Wainwright

Barrow

ARCTIC COASTAL PLAIN

CHUKCHI SEA

Point Hope

BROOKS RANGE

RUSSIA

Kotzebue Sound

Kotzebue

Yukon

CANADA

GULF OF
ANADYR

Gambell

Nome

Norton Sound

St. Lawrence
Island

Unalakleet

Fairbanks

ALASKA

Mt. McKinley

ALASKA RANGE

BERING SEA

St. Matthew
Island

Cape Romanzof

Nunivak
Island

Hooper Bay

Bethel

Anchorage

Cordova

Yakutat

ALEXANDER
ARCHIPELAGO

Cape Newenham

Dillingham

GULF OF ALASKA

St. Paul Island

BRISTOL
BAY

Kodiak

Kodiak Island

Chignik

Trinity Islands

Chirikof Island

St. George Island

Fort Randall

Shumagin Islands

Unimak Island

Sanak Island

A L E U T I A N   I S L A N D S

Dutch Harbor

Rat Islands

Andreanof Islands

Fox Islands

HAWAIIAN ISLANDS (USA)

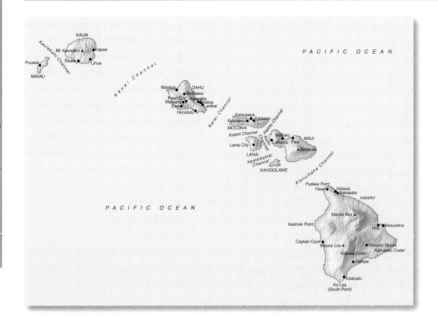

UNITED STATES

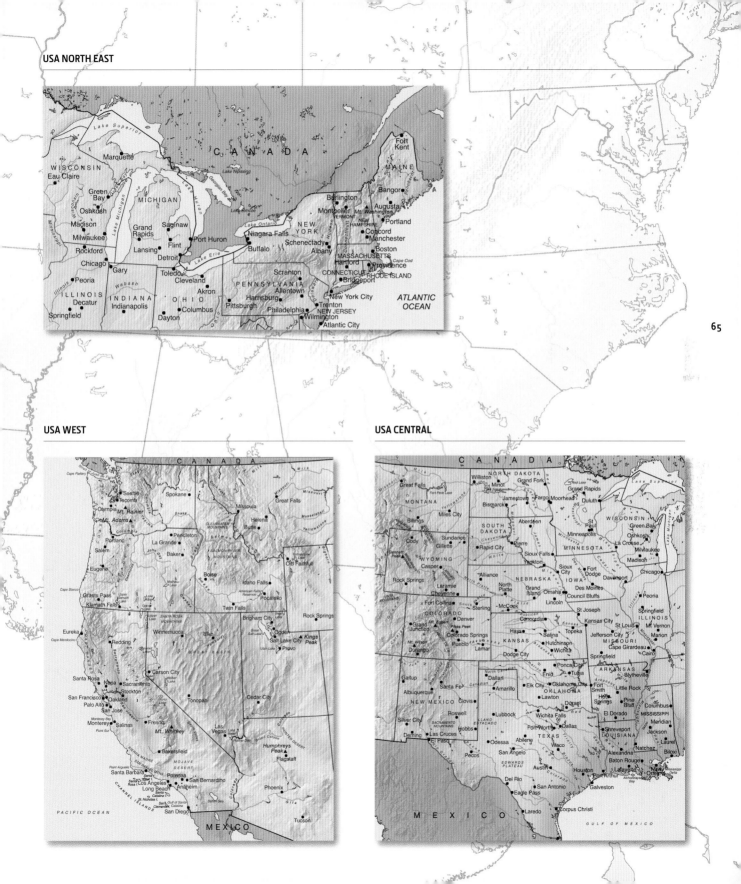

USA NORTH EAST

USA WEST

USA CENTRAL

USA EAST

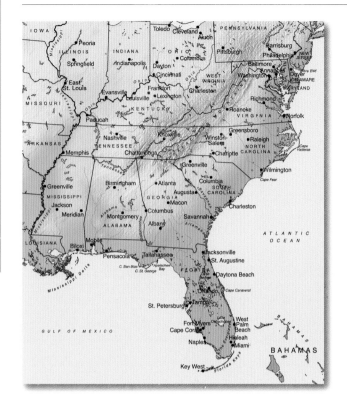

MEXICO

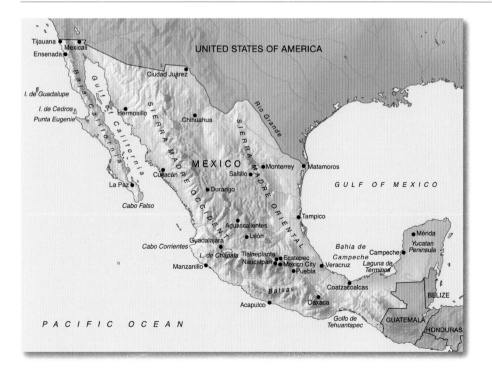

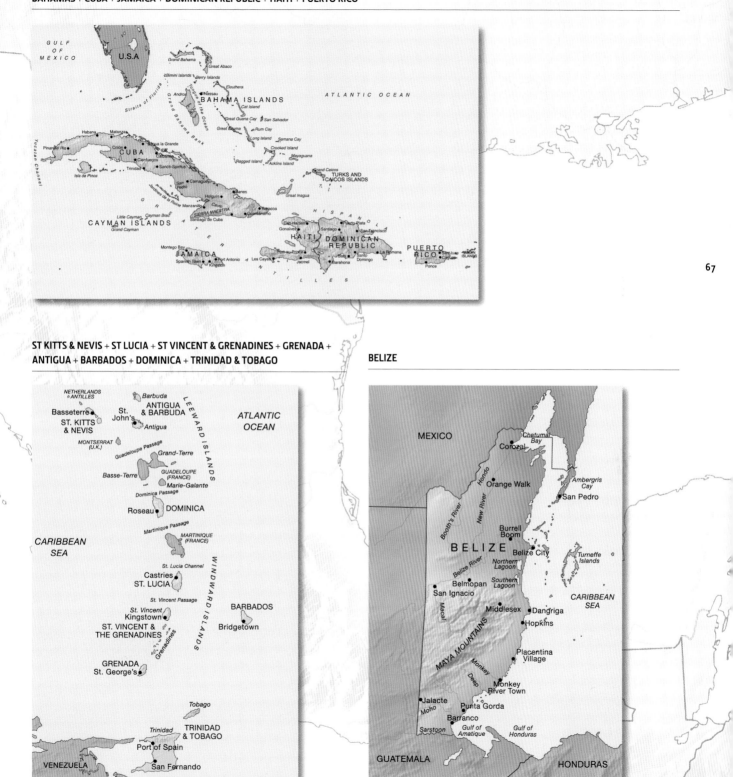

BAHAMAS + CUBA + JAMAICA + DOMINICAN REPUBLIC + HAITI + PUERTO RICO

GULF OF MEXICO

U.S.A

Grand Bahama

Great Abaco

Bimini Islands

Berry Islands

Eleuthera

ATLANTIC OCEAN

Nassau

BAHAMA ISLANDS

Cat Island

Andros

San Salvador

Great Guana Cay

Great Exuma

Rum Cay

Straits of Florida

Long Island

Samana Cay

Grand Bahama Bank

Crooked Island

Yucatan Channel

Habana

Matanzas

Ragged Island

Mayaguana

Acklins Island

Pinar del Rio

Colon

Sagua la Grande

CUBA

Cabanas

Cienfuegos

Santa Clara

Isla de Pinos

Trinidad

Sancti-Spiritus

Grand Caicos

TURKS AND CAICOS ISLANDS

San Pedro

Camaguey

Holguin

Banes

Jardines de la Reina

Caudo

Great Inagua

HISPANIOLA

Little Cayman

Cayman Brac

Manzanillo

SIERRA MAESTRA

Baracoa

Cap-Haitien

Puerto-Plata

San Francisco

CAYMAN ISLANDS

Santiago de Cuba

Guantanamo

Gonaives

Santiago

PUERTO RICO

Grand Cayman

Montego Bay

HAITI

DOMINICAN REPUBLIC

La Romana

San Juan

VIRGIN ISLANDS

JAMAICA

Spanish Town

Port Antonio

Les Cayes

Port-au-Prince

Bani

Santo Domingo

Ponce

Kingston

Jacmel

Barahona

GREATER ANTILLES

67

ST KITTS & NEVIS + ST LUCIA + ST VINCENT & GRENADINES + GRENADA + ANTIGUA + BARBADOS + DOMINICA + TRINIDAD & TOBAGO

NETHERLANDS ANTILLES

Barbuda

ANTIGUA & BARBUDA

ATLANTIC OCEAN

Basseterre

St. John's

ST. KITTS & NEVIS

Antigua

LEEWARD ISLANDS

MONTSERRAT (U.K.)

Guadeloupe Passage

Grand-Terre

Basse-Terre

GUADELOUPE (FRANCE)

Marie-Galante

Dominica Passage

Roseau

DOMINICA

CARIBBEAN SEA

Martinique Passage

MARTINIQUE (FRANCE)

St. Lucia Channel

Castries

ST. LUCIA

WINDWARD ISLANDS

St. Vincent Passage

BARBADOS

St. Vincent

Kingstown

ST. VINCENT & THE GRENADINES

Bridgetown

Grenadines

GRENADA

St. George's

Tobago

Trinidad

TRINIDAD & TOBAGO

VENEZUELA

Port of Spain

San Fernando

BELIZE

MEXICO

Chetumal Bay

Corozal

Hondo

Ambergris Cay

Orange Walk

Booth's River

New River

San Pedro

Burrell Boom

BELIZE

Belize City

Turneffe Islands

Belize River

Northern Lagoon

Belmopan

Southern Lagoon

San Ignacio

CARIBBEAN SEA

Macal

Middlesex

Dangriga

Hopkins

MAYA MOUNTAINS

Placentina Village

Monkey

Deep

Monkey River Town

Jalacte

Moho

Punta Gorda

Barranco

Sarstoon

Gulf of Amatique

Gulf of Honduras

GUATEMALA

HONDURAS

GUATEMALA

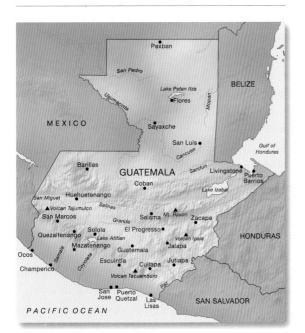

HONDURAS

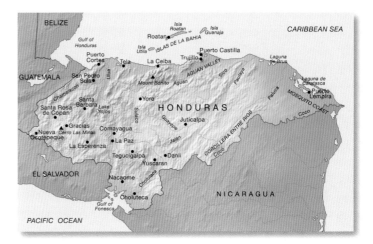

NICARAGUA

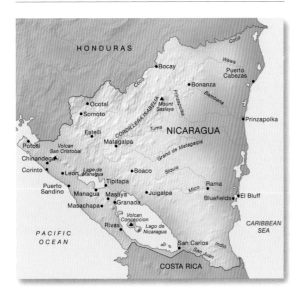

EL SALVADOR

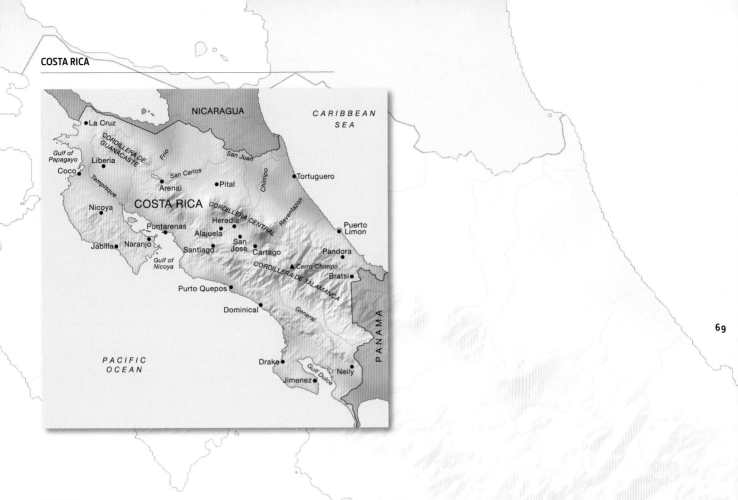

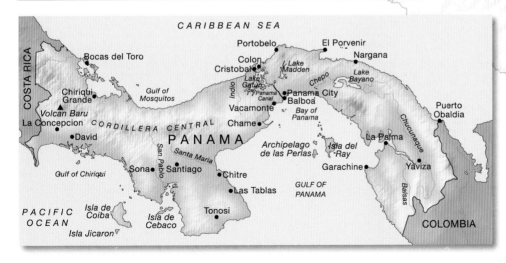

VENEZUELA

CARIBBEAN SEA

BARBADOS

Netherlands Antilles

Punto Fijo

GRENADA

Paraguaipoa

Coro

La Asuncion

Marácaibo

Cabimas   Tocuyo

Caracas

TRINIDAD
AND
TOBAGO

Valencia   Cumana

Lake
Maracaibo   Barquisimeto   Mt. Platillon   Barcelona

▲ Pico Bolivar   VENEZUELA   Maturin

Tucupita

Orinoco   Ciudad
Guyana

San Cristobal   Apure   Ciudad
Bolivar

Arauca   Caicara   Tumeremo

Meta   Caura   Caroni   Angel
Falls   GUYANA

Puerto Ayacucho   Paragua

GUIANA HIGHLANDS
Ventuari   Santa Elena

COLOMBIA

Orinoco

San Carlos de
Rio Negro

BRAZIL

COLOMBIA

CARIBBEAN
SEA   Pta. Gallinas

Barranquilla   Gulf of
Venezuela

Valledupar

PANAMA

VENEZUELA

Gulf of
Panama

Magdalena   Cauca

Cabo
Corrientes

Arauca

Medellin   LLANOS

Meta

Pereira   Manizales

Nevado del Tolima ▲   Bogotá

Buenaventura   Armenia   Ibague

Cali • ANDES
MOUNTAINS   COLOMBIA   Gauviare

▲   Neiva

Nevado
del Huila

Mocoa   Mitu

ECUADOR

Caquetá

PERU   BRAZIL

GUYANA + SURINAME + FRENCH GUIANA

Morawhanna   NORTH ATLANTIC OCEAN

VENEZUELA

Charity

Georgetown

Enmore

Bartica   New Amsterdam

Issano   Paramaribo   Saint-Laurent
du-Moroni

PAKARAIMA
MTS.   Linden   Nieuw
Nickerie   Totness   Albina   Sinnamary

Mahida   Brokopondo   Cayenne

GUYANA   Bitagron   W.J. van
Blommestein
Lake   Maria   Kaw

▲

Hendrick Top   Saul

Kumaka   Suriname   FRENCH
GUIANA

Pirara   SURINAME

Essequibo

Biloku

BRAZIL

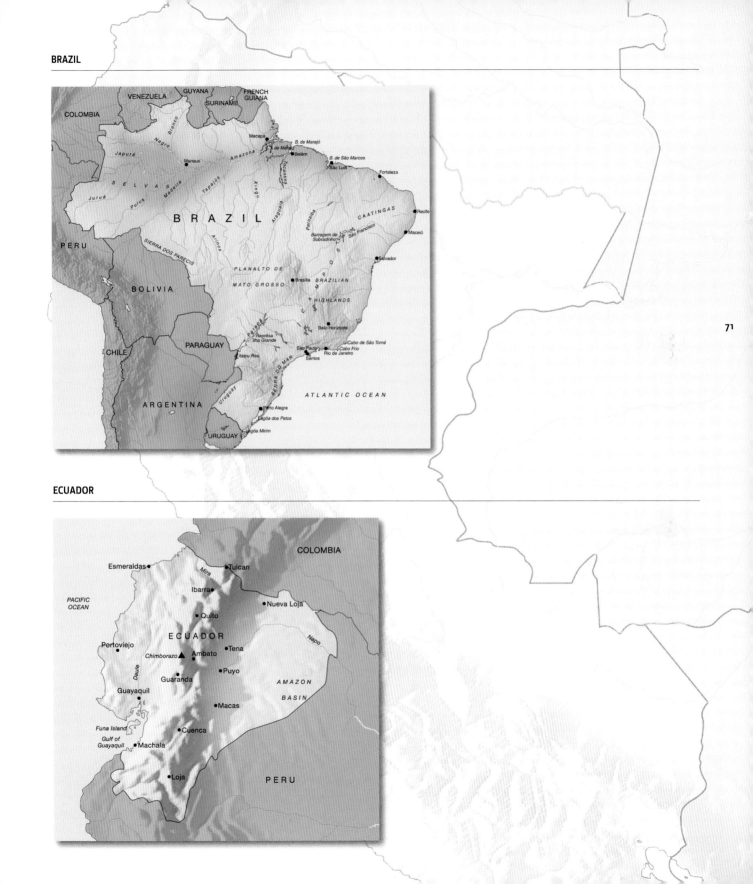

PERU

BOLIVIA

PARAGUAY

URUGUAY

ARGENTINA

BRAZIL

Artigas

Rivera

HAEDO HILLS

Salto

Tacuarembo

Uruguay

San Gregorio

Negro

Melo

Paysandu

Embalse del
Rio Negro

Rio Branco

Negro

Tacuari

GRANDE RANGE

Cebollanti

Dolores

Trinidad

Lascano

Muerta

Chuy

Florida

Santa Lucia

Minas

Mount Catredal

Castillos

Carmelo

San Jose

Pando

Rocha

Colonia

Montevideo

San Carlos

Maldonado

Rio de la Plata

ATLANTIC
OCEAN

CHILE

PERU

BOLIVIA

Arica

Iquique

Atacama Desert

Antofagasta

CHILE

Copiapo

Coquimbo

PACIFIC
OCEAN

Valparaiso

Santiago

ARGENTINA

Concepcion

Temuco

Valdivia

Peurto Aisen

Cerro San Valentin

ATLANTIC
OCEAN

Gulf of Penas

Strait of Magellan

Punta Arenas

Tierra
del Fuego

Cape Horn

73

ARGENTINA

ICELAND

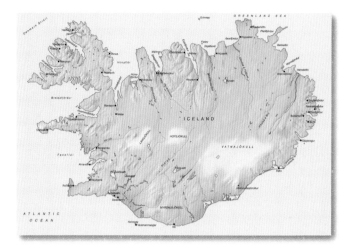

NORWAY

FINLAND

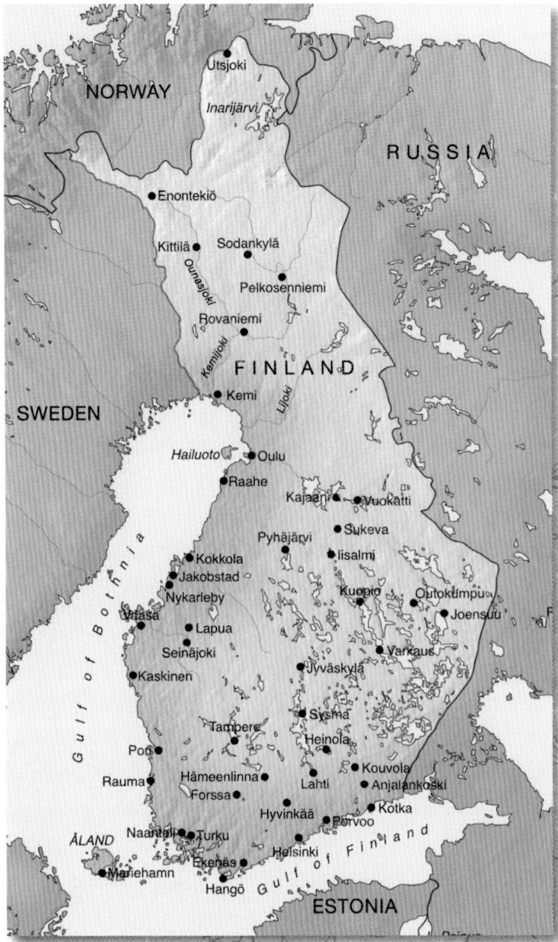
NORWAY
Utsjoki
Inarijärvi
RUSSIA
Enontekiö
Kittilä
Sodankylä
Ounasjoki
Pelkosenniemi
Rovaniemi
Kemijoki
FINLAND
Kemi
Iijoki
SWEDEN
Hailuoto
Oulu
Raahe
Kajaani
Vuokatti
Sukeva
Pyhäjärvi
Iisalmi
Kokkola
Jakobstad
Nykarleby
Kuopio
Outokumpu
Joensuu
Vaasa
Lapua
Seinäjoki
Varkaus
Kaskinen
Jyväskylä
Sysmä
Tampere
Heinola
Pori
Kouvola
Rauma
Hämeenlinna
Lahti
Anjalankoski
Forssa
Kotka
Hyvinkää
Porvoo
ÅLAND
Naantali
Turku
Helsinki
Ekenäs
Mariehamn
Hangö
Gulf of Bothnia
Gulf of Finland
ESTONIA

SWEDEN

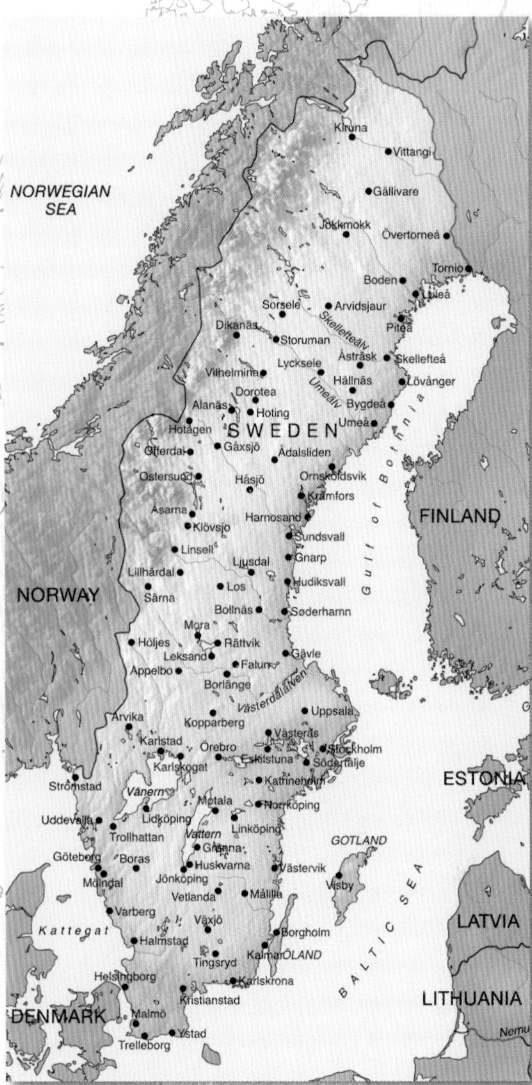
NORWEGIAN SEA
Kiruna
Vittangi
Gällivare
Jokkmokk
Övertorneå
Tornio
Boden
Luleå
Sorsele
Arvidsjaur
Piteå
Dikanäs
Storuman
Skellefteälv
Åstråsk
Skellefteå
Vilhelmina
Lycksele
Hällnäs
Lövånger
Dorotea
Umeälv
Bygdeå
Alanäs
Hoting
Umeå
Hotagen
SWEDEN
Offerdal
Gäxsjö
Ådalsliden
Östersund
Häsjö
Örnsköldsvik
Kramfors
Åsarna
Härnösand
FINLAND
Klövsjo
Sundsvall
Linsell
Gnarp
Ljusdal
Lillhärdal
Hudiksvall
NORWAY
Särna
Los
Bollnäs
Söderhamn
Gulf of Bothnia
Mora
Höljes
Rättvik
Gävle
Leksand
Falun
Appelbo
Borlänge
Västerdalälven
Arvika
Kopparberg
Uppsala
Västerås
Karlstad
Örebro
Stockholm
Eskilstuna
Södertälje
Karlskogat
Strömstad
ESTONIA
Vänern
Katrineholm
Uddevalla
Motala
Norrköping
Lidköping
Trollhattan
Vättern
Linköping
GOTLAND
Gränna
Göteborg
Boras
Huskvarna
Västervik
Mölndal
Jönköping
Visby
Vetlanda
Målilla
Varberg
Växjö
LATVIA
Kattegat
Borgholm
Halmstad
Tingsryd
Kalmar
ÖLAND
BALTIC SEA
Helsingborg
Karlskrona
Kristianstad
LITHUANIA
DENMARK
Malmö
Ystad
Trelleborg

UNITED KINGDOM

IRELAND

ESTONIA

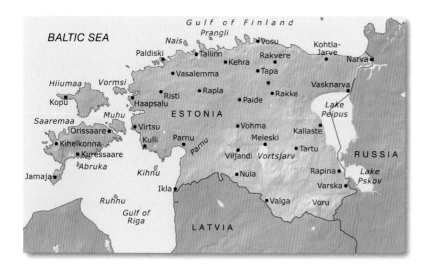

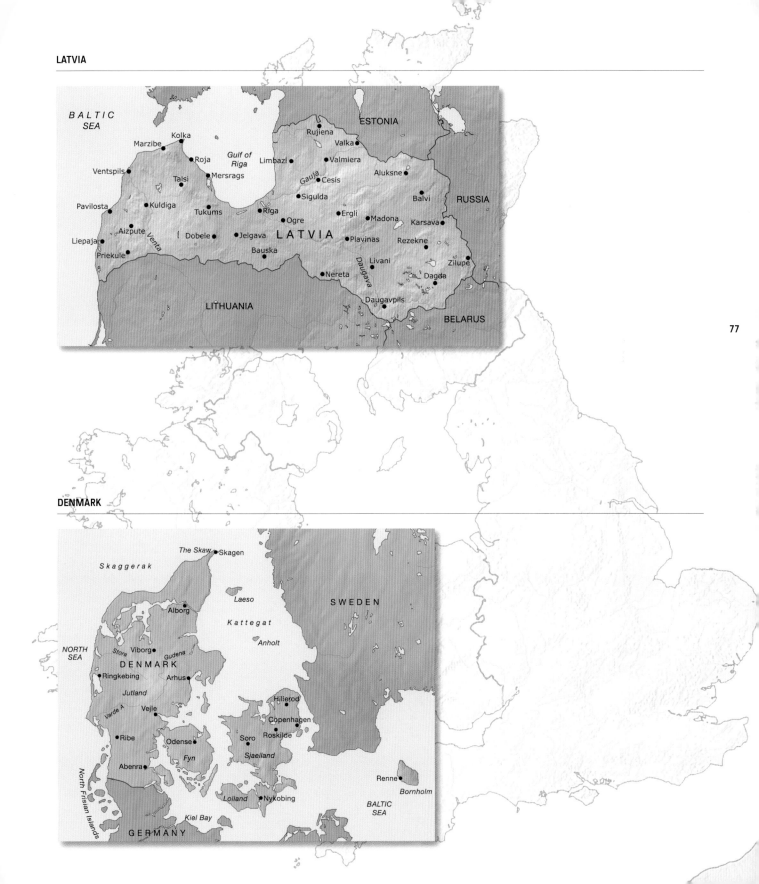

LATVIA

BALTIC
SEA

ESTONIA

Kolka
Marzibe
Roja
Gulf of
Riga
Limbazi
Rujiena
Valka
Valmiera
Aluksne
Ventspils
Talsi
Mersrags
Gauja
Cesis
Pavilosta
Kuldiga
Tukums
Sigulda
Balvi
Riga
Ergli
Madona
Karsava
Aizpute
Dobele
Jelgava
Ogre
Plavinas
Rezekne
Liepaja
Priekule
Venta
Bauska
Livani
Zilupe
Nereta
Daugava
Dagda
Daugavpils
LATVIA
RUSSIA
LITHUANIA
BELARUS

77

DENMARK

The Skaw
Skagen
Skaggerak
Laeso
SWEDEN
Alborg
Kattegat
Anholt
NORTH
SEA
Stora
Viborg
Gudena
DENMARK
Ringkebing
Arhus
Jutland
Hilierod
Varde A
Vejle
Copenhagen
Ribe
Odense
Soro
Roskilde
Fyn
Sjaelland
Abenra
Renne
Bornholm
North Frisian Islands
Lolland
Nykobing
BALTIC
SEA
Kiel Bay
GERMANY

LITHUANIA

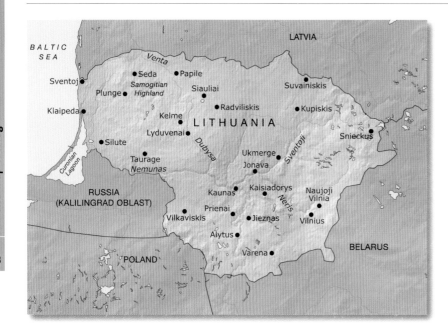

BELARUS

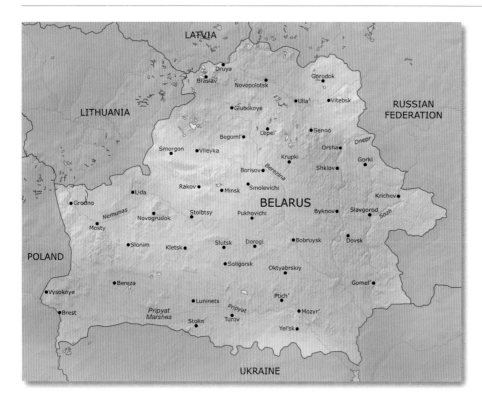

GERMANY

POLAND

NETHERLANDS

UKRAINE + MOLDOVA

BELGIUM + LUXEMBOURG

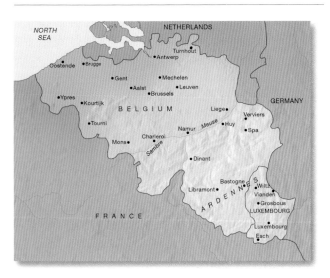

FRANCE + MONACO

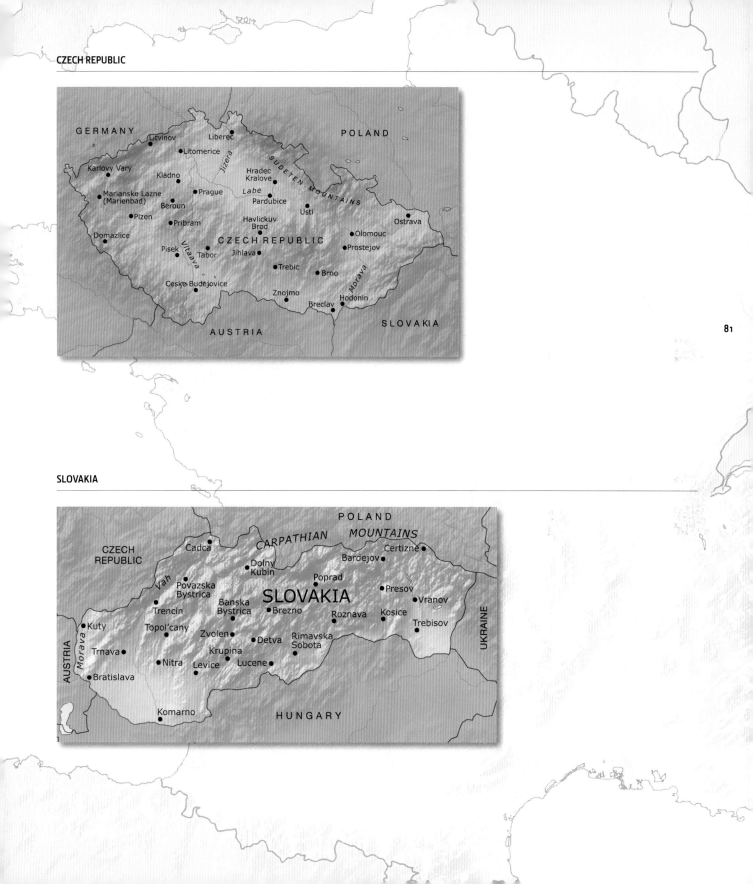

AUSTRIA

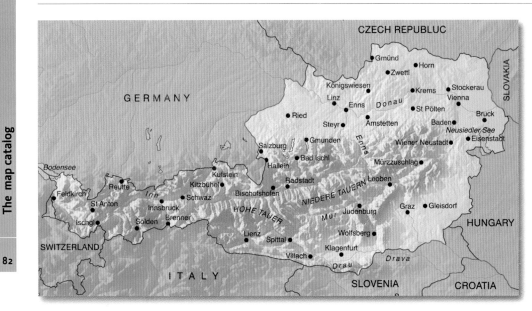

HUNGARY

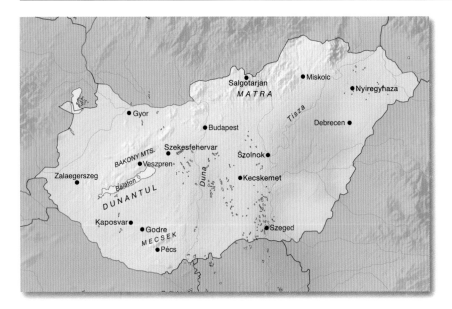

FRANCE

Schaffhausen • Konstanz
Basel • • Bodensee
Porrentruy • Baden • Frauenfeld
Delémont • Liestal • Winterthur • St Gallen
Olten • Aarau • Zurich • Herisau
Solothurn • • Appenzell
Neuchâtel • Burgdorf • Walenstadt • LIECHTENSTEIN
Lac de Neuchâtel • Luzern • Zug • • Vaduz
Bern • Sarnen • Schwyz • Glarus
Fribourg • Thun • Brienz • Altdorf • Linthal • Chur • Klosters
Vallorbe • Yverdon • Bulle • Interlaken • Andermatt • Laax • Davos • Scuol
Morges • Lausanne • Lenk ▲ Finsteraarhorn • SWITZERLAND • Zernez
Lac Léman • Montreux • BERNER ALPEN • Rhône • ALPI LEPONTINE • St Moritz
Aigle • Sion • Sierre • St Moritz
Martigny • Zermatt • Bellinzona
▲ Mont Blanc • ▲ Matterhorn • Locarno
▲ Monte Rosa • Lugano

SWITZERLAND

ITALY

UKRAINE

Darabani •
Satu Mare • Solotvina • Radauti •
Carei • Baia Mare • Borsa • • Botosani
HUNGARY Tasnad • Vatra-Dornei • Pascani • Iasi
Oradea • Somes • Dej • Bistrita • CARPATHIAN MOUNTAINS MOLDOVA
Cluj-Napoca • Mures • • Husi
Chisineu Cris • Turda • Tirgu Mures • Bistrita • Bacau
Vascau • Bistra • Sighisoara • Tirgu-Ocna • • Birlad
Arad • Alba Iulia • Mercurea-Ciuc •
Nadlac • Mures • Medias • • Tecuci
Timisoara • Faget • Deva • Sebes • Sibiu • Fagaras • Sfintu Gheorghe • Focsani
Lugoj • Hunedoara • ROMANIA • Brasov • Galati
Timis • Petrosani • ▲ Moldoveanu • Braila • Cerna • Sulina
Caransebes • TRANSYLVANIAN ALPS • ▲ Omu • Buzau • Faurei
Resita • Verendin • Tirgu Jiu • Rimnicu Vilcea • Buzau • Babadag
Bazias • Drobeta-Turnu Severin • Olt • Ploiesti • Upziceni • Mouths of the Danube
SERBIA • Dragasani • Pitesti • Tirgoviste • Slobozia •
Filiesi • Jiu • Slatina • Ialomita • Fetesti
Craiova • Bucharest • Calarasi • Constanta
Dunav • Caracal • Giurgiu • Dunav (Danube) • BLACK SEA
Alexandria • • Mangalia

BULGARIA

SPAIN + ANDORRA

ITALY + MALTA + SAN MARINO + VATICAN CITY

SLOVENIA

CROATIA

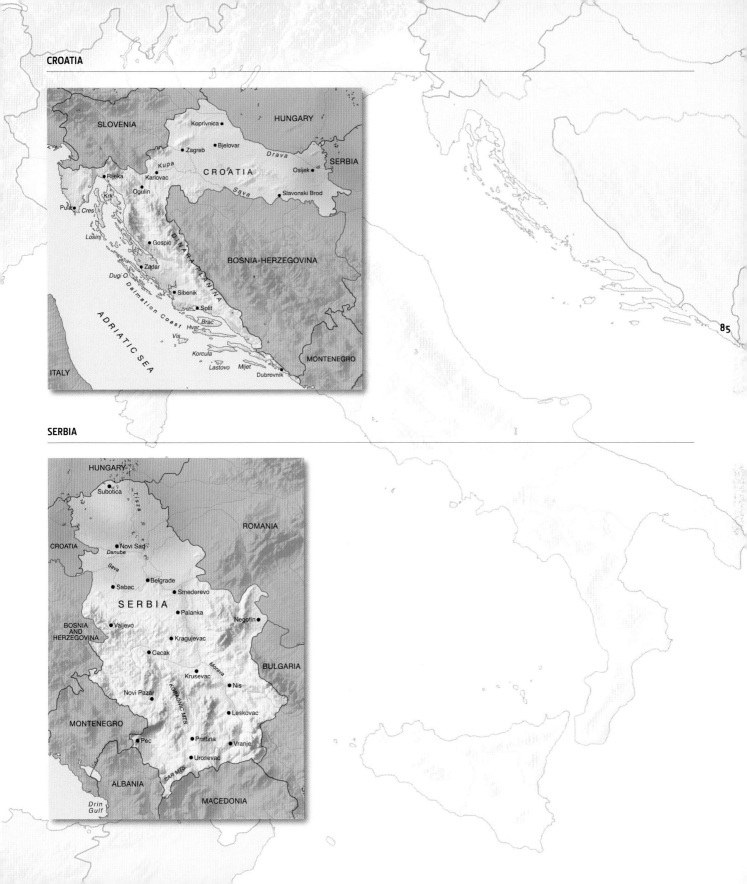

SLOVENIA

HUNGARY

Koprivnica

Bjelovar

Zagreb

Drava

SERBIA

Kupa

C R O A T I A

Osijek

Rijeka

Karlovac

Ogulin

Sava

Slavonski Brod

Krk

Pula

Cres

Losinj

Gospic

DINARA PLANINA

BOSNIA-HERZEGOVINA

Zadar

Dugi O.

Dalmatian Coast

Sibenik

Split

Brac

Hvar

Vis

Korcula

Lastovo

Mljet

MONTENEGRO

ADRIATIC SEA

ITALY

Dubrovnik

85

SERBIA

HUNGARY

Subotica

Tisza

ROMANIA

CROATIA

Novi Sad

Danube

Sava

Belgrade

Sabac

Smederevo

S E R B I A

Palanka

Negotin

Valjevo

BOSNIA
AND
HERZEGOVINA

Kragujevac

Cacak

Morava

BULGARIA

Krusevac

Nis

Novi Pazar

KOPAONIC MTS.

Leskovac

MONTENEGRO

Pec

Pristina

Vranje

Urosevac

SAR MTS.

ALBANIA

MACEDONIA

Drin
Gulf

PORTUGAL

MONTENEGRO

BOSNIA-HERZEGOVINA

CROATIA
Bosanski Novi
Prijedor
Bihac
Omarska
Derventa
Banja Luka
Brcko
SERBIA
Teslic
Tuzla
Sana
Una
Drvar
BOSNIA-HERZEGOVINA
Zvornik
Zenica
Kladanj
Vrbas
Vares
Bosna
Livno
Sarajevo
Visegrad
Konjic
Drina
Mt. Plocno
Foca
Neretva
Mostar
DINARIC ALPS
CROATIA
Dalmation Coast
Bileca
Trebinje
MONTENEGRO
ADRIATIC SEA

ALBANIA

MONTENEGRO
SERBIA
NORTH ALBANIAN ALPS
Lake Scutari
Drin
Shkoder
Kashnjet
KORAB MTNS.
Drin Gulf
Lezhe
Peshkopi
Durres
MACEDONIA
Tirane
Kavaje
Elbassan
ALBANIA
Lake Ohrid
Lushnje
ADRIATIC SEA
Kucove
Pogradec
Lake Prespa
Fier
Berat
Deboll
Korce
Vlore
Ostum
Palase
Vijose
PINDUS MTNS.
Gjirokaster
Butrint
Jergucat
Lukove
GREECE

87

BULGARIA

Dunav
ROMANIA
Dunav (Danube)
Silistra
Vidin
Lom
Ruse
Dobrich
Svishtov
Balchik
Pleven
Popovo
Novi Pazar
Vraca
Iskur
Lovech
Varna
STARA
Turgovishte
Kostinbrod
BULGARIA
SERBIA
PLANINA
Sofia
Botev
Kazanluk
Sliven
Pernik
Kalovo
Tundza
BLACK SEA
Yambol
Burgas
StaraZagora
Musala
Pasardzhik
Chirpan
Velingrad
Dimitrovgrad
RHODOPE
Plovdiv
Marica
Bansko
Mt. Vikhren
Golyam Perelik
PIRIN MTS.
Struma
Smolyan
Kardzali
MACEDONIA
MOUNTAINS
TURKEY
GREECE

MACEDONIA

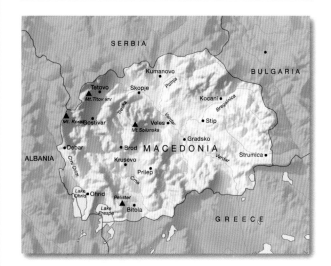

CYPRUS

GREECE

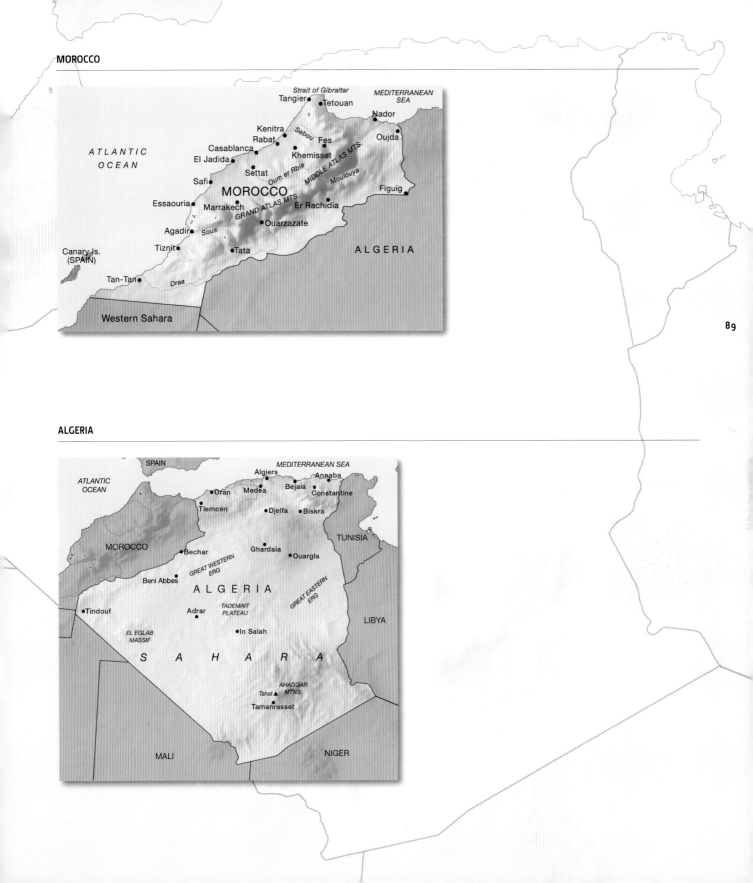

ALGERIA

TUNISIA

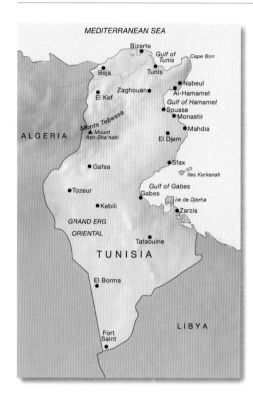

LIBYA

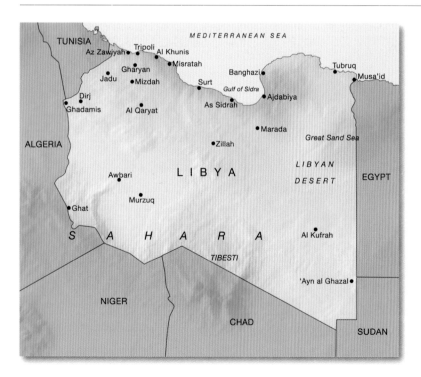

EGYPT

MEDITERRANEAN SEA

Marsa Matruh
Alexandria
Damietta
Port Said
ISRAEL
JORDAN
Al Mansurah
Suez Canal
Az Zagazig
Giza
Cairo
Suez
Pyramids of Giza
Al Fayyum
QATTARA DEPRESSION
Sinai Peninsula
SAUDI ARABIA
Al Minya
Dayrut
ARABIAN DESERT
Asyut
Nile
EGYPT
LIBYA
Qina
RED SEA
Naj Al Karijah
Thebes
Al Karnak
Luxor
Valley of the Kings
LIBYAN DESERT
KARIJAH OASIS
ARABIAN DESERT
Aswan High Dam
Aswan
Lake Nasser
Abu Simbel
SUDAN

MALI

ALGERIA
Taoudenni
S A H A R A
MAURITANIA
MALI
ADRAR DES IFORAS
Tombouctou
Bourem
Niger
Gao
Mepaka
Nara
Mopti
DOGON PLATEAU
Kayes
Koro
Balfoulabe
NIGER
Segou
Bamako
Kangaba
BURKINA FASO
Sikasso
GUINEA
COTE D'IVOIRE

MAURITANIA + CAPE VERDE IS + WESTERN SAHARA

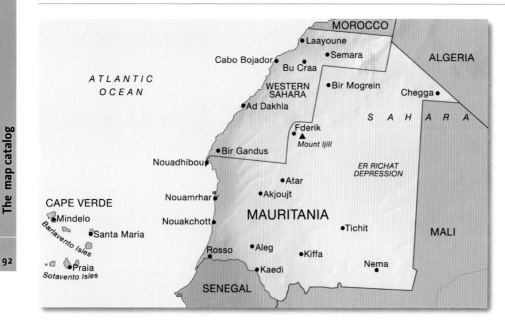

NIGER

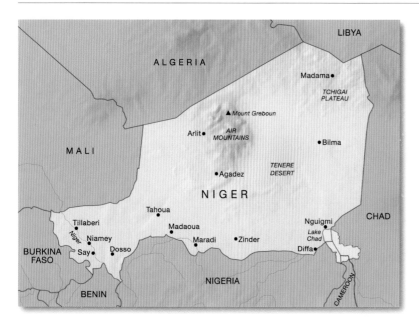

CHAD

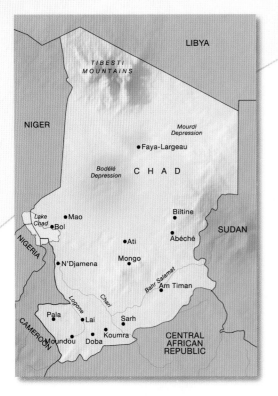

CHAD

LIBYA

TIBESTI
MOUNTAINS

NIGER

Mourdi
Depression

Faya-Largeau

Bodélé
Depression

CHAD

SUDAN

Lake
Chad • Mao
Bol

Biltine

NIGERIA

N'Djamena

Ati

Mongo

Abéché

Bahr Salamat

Am Timan

CAMEROON

Pala

Lai

Koumra

Sarh

Moundou

Doba

Logone

Chari

CENTRAL
AFRICAN
REPUBLIC

SUDAN

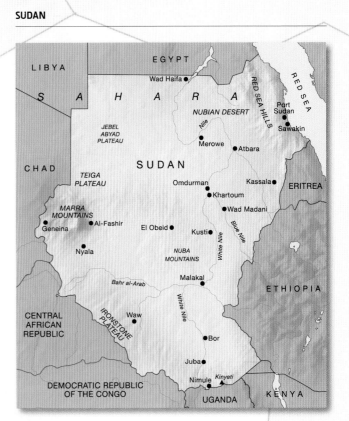

SUDAN

LIBYA

EGYPT

Wad Haifa

RED SEA

S A H A R A

NUBIAN DESERT

RED SEA HILLS

Port
Sudan

Sawakin

CHAD

JEBEL
ABYAD
PLATEAU

Nile

Merowe

Atbara

S U D A N

TEIGA
PLATEAU

MARRA
MOUNTAINS

Geneina

Al-Fashir

Omdurman

Khartoum

Kassala

ERITREA

Wad Madani

El Obeid

Kusti

Nyala

NUBA
MOUNTAINS

Bahr al-Arab

Malakal

White Nile

Blue Nile

ETHIOPIA

CENTRAL
AFRICAN
REPUBLIC

IRONSTONE
PLATEAU

Waw

White Nile

Bor

Juba

Nimule

Kinyeti

DEMOCRATIC REPUBLIC
OF THE CONGO

UGANDA

K E N Y A

93

GAMBIA + SENEGAL

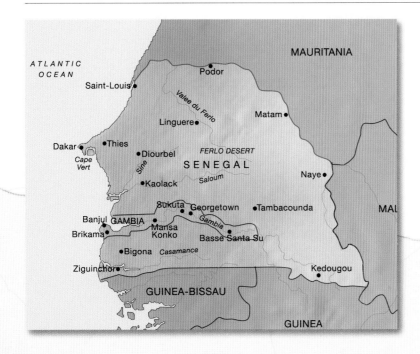

MAURITANIA

ATLANTIC
OCEAN

Podor

Saint-Louis

Valee du Ferlo

Matam

Dakar

Linguere

Thies

FERLO DESERT

Cape
Vert

Diourbel

SENEGAL

Sine

Naye

MAL

Kaolack

Saloum

Sukuta

Georgetown

Tambacounda

Banjul

GAMBIA

Gambia

Brikama

Mansa
Konko

Basse Santa Su

Bigona

Casamance

Ziguinchor

Kedougou

GUINEA-BISSAU

GUINEA

ERITREA

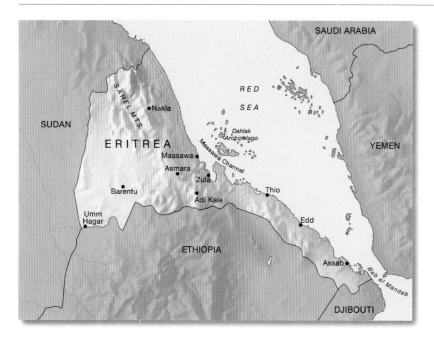

BURKINA FASO + IVORY COAST + GHANA + TOGO + BENIN

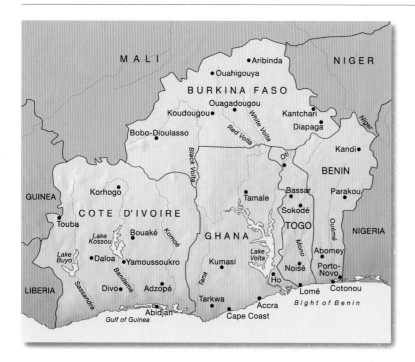

ETHIOPIA

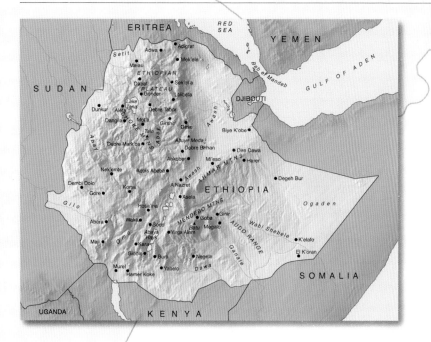

ERITREA
RED SEA
YEMEN
Sefit
Adwa
Adigrat
Maiau
Mek'ele
ETHIOPIAN
Sek'ot'a
SUDAN
Dabat
Gonder
Lalibela
PLATEAU
DJIBOUTI
Dunkur
Alefa
Debre Tabor
Lake
Tana
Mota
Dangila
Girshit
Dese
Awash
Biye K'obe
Talo
Debre Mark'os
Apuye Meda
Abay
Debre Birhan
Dire Dawa
Ankober
Mieso
Harer
Nek'emte
Addis Abeba
Awash
Dembi Dolo
Gore
Koma
A Nazret
Degeh Bur
Hosa'ina
Asela
ETHIOPIA
Ogaden
Abera
Waka
Goba
Ginir
Sodo
Batu
Megalo
Wabi Shebele
Maji
Abiya
Hayk
Virga Alem
AUDO RANGE
K'elafo
Gidole
Kara
Burji
MENDEBO MTNS
Murel
Negele
Yabelo
El K'oran
Hamer Koke
Dawa
Ganale
SOMALIA
UGANDA
KENYA

95

DJIBOUTI

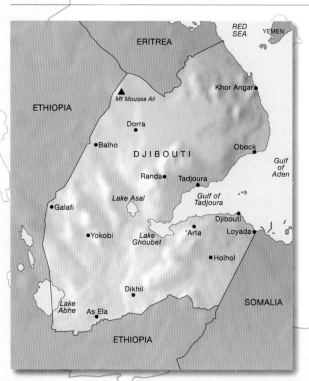

ERITREA
RED SEA
YEMEN
▲ Mt Moussa Ali
Khor Angar
ETHIOPIA
Dorra
Balho
Obock
DJIBOUTI
Randa
Tadjoura
Gulf of Aden
Lake Asal
Gulf of Tadjoura
Galafi
Djibouti
'Arta
Loyada
Yokobi
Lake Ghoubet
Holhol
Dikhil
Lake Abhe
As Ela
SOMALIA
ETHIOPIA

GUINEA + GUINEA BISSAU + LIBERIA + SIERRA LEONE

SENEGAL
Cacheu
Farim
Gabu
MALI
Bissau
Geba
Bafata
Mali
GUINEA BISSAU
Gaoual
FOUTA DJALON
Siguiri
BIJAGOS ISLANDS
Catio
Boke
Pita
Dabola
Baling
GUINEA
Mamou
Niger
Kankan
Boffa
Kabala
Faranah
Milo
Conakry
Kambia
Kissidougou
Lungi
Makeni
Beyla
Freetown
SIERRA LEONE
Shenge
Bo
Sewa
Nzerekore
Kenema
Zorzor
Mount Nimba ▲
COTE D'IVOIRE
Sherbro Island
ATLANTIC OCEAN
Robertsport
Kle
Saint Paul
Monrovia
LIBERIA
Zwedru
Buchanan
Cestos
Greenville
Grand Cess
Harper

NIGERIA

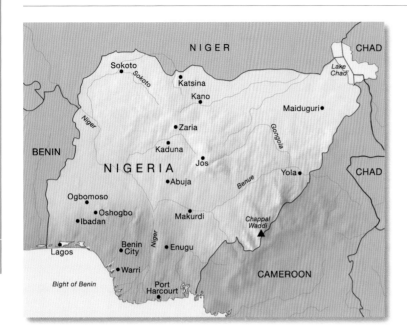

NIGER

CHAD

Sokoto
Sokoto

Katsina

Kano

Maiduguri

Lake Chad

Zaria

Niger

Kaduna

Jos

Gongola

Yola

CHAD

BENIN

NIGERIA

Abuja

Benue

Ogbomoso

Oshogbo

Ibadan

Makurdi

Chappal Waddi ▲

Lagos

Benin City

Niger

Enugu

Warri

CAMEROON

Bight of Benin

Port Harcourt

SOMALIA

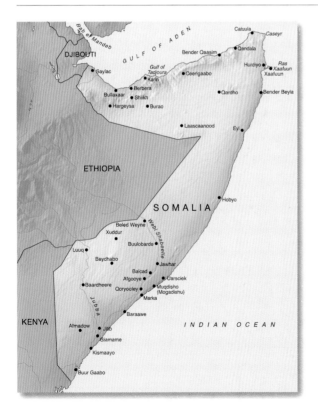

Bab el Mandeb

GULF OF ADEN

Caluula

Caseyr

DJIBOUTI

Bender Qaasim

Qandala

Saylac

Gulf of Tadjoura

Karin

Ceerigaabo

Hurdiyo

Ras Xaafuun

Xaafuun

Berbera

Bullaxaar

Shiikh

Qardho

Bender Beyla

Hargeysa

Burao

Laascaanood

Eyl

ETHIOPIA

SOMALIA

Hobyo

Beled Weyne

Wabi Shabeelle

Xuddur

Buulobarde

Luuq

Baydhabo

Jawhar

Balcad

Afgooye

Uarsciek

Baardheere

Qoryooley

Muqdisho (Mogadishu)

Marka

Jubba

Baraawe

KENYA

Afmadow

Jilib

INDIAN OCEAN

Giamame

Kismaayo

Buur Gaabo

CAMEROON

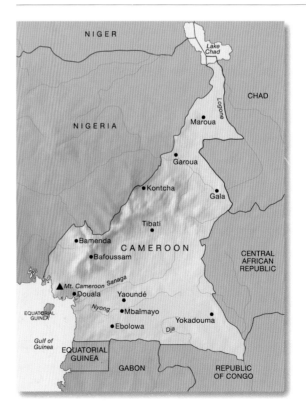

NIGER

Lake Chad

CHAD

NIGERIA

Logone

Maroua

Garoua

Kontcha

Gala

Tibati

Bamenda

CAMEROON

CENTRAL AFRICAN REPUBLIC

Bafoussam

▲ Mt. Cameroon

Sanaga

Douala

Yaoundé

EQUATORIAL GUINEA

Nyong

Mbalmayo

Yokadouma

Ebolowa

Dja

Gulf of Guinea

EQUATORIAL GUINEA

GABON

REPUBLIC OF CONGO

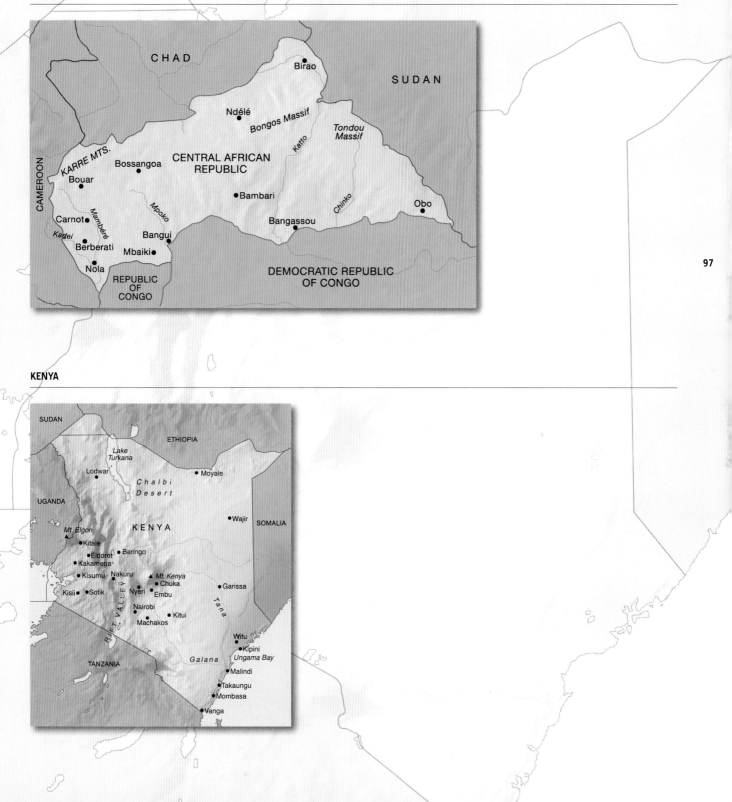

CHAD

Birao

SUDAN

Ndélé

Bongos Massif

Tondou
Massif

KARRE MTS.

Katto

CENTRAL AFRICAN
REPUBLIC

Bossangoa

CAMEROON

Bouar

Bambari

Chinko

Obo

Mambéré

Mpoko

Carnot

Kadei

Bangui

Bangassou

Berberati

Mbaiki

Nola

REPUBLIC
OF
CONGO

DEMOCRATIC REPUBLIC
OF CONGO

97

SUDAN

ETHIOPIA

Lake
Turkana

Lodwar

Moyale

Chalbi
Desert

UGANDA

Wajir

SOMALIA

Mt. Elgon

KENYA

Kitale

Eldoret

Baringo

Kakamega

Kisumu

Nakuru

Mt. Kenya

Chuka

Garissa

Kisii

Sotik

Nyeri

Embu

Tana

Nairobi

Kitui

Machakos

RIFT VALLEY

Witu

Kipini

Ungama Bay

Galana

Malindi

TANZANIA

Takaungu

Mombasa

Vanga

UGANDA

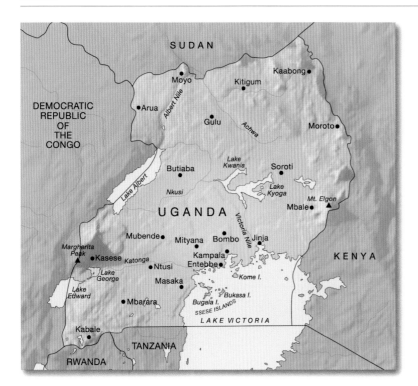

EQUATORIAL GUINEA + GABON + SAOTOME & PRINCIPE + CONGO (REPUBLIC OF)

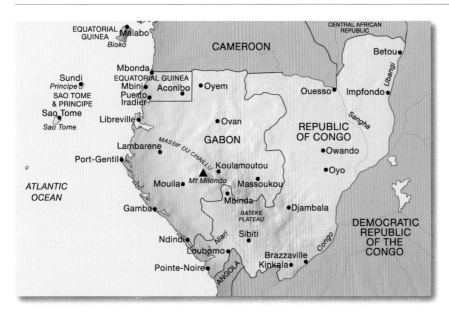

CONGO (DEMOCRATIC REPUBLIC OF)

CENTRAL AFRICAN REPUBLIC
SUDAN
CAMEROON
Bomu
Bondo
Uele
Lisala
Mungbere
Lake Albert
Congo
GABON
REPUBLIC
OF
CONGO
Kisangani
Lake Edward UGANDA
Mbandaka
Lake
Tumba
Lomami
Goma
DEMOCRATIC
REPUBLIC
OF THE
CONGO
Lake
Mai-Ndombe
Lake Kivu RWANDA
Bukavu
Fimi
Kindu
BURUNDI
Bandundu
Kasai
Lualaba
Kinshasa
Sankuru
MITUMBA MOUNTAINS
TANZANIA
Matadi
Kananga
Mbuji-Mayi
Kalemie
Lubilash
Lake
Tanganyika
Kasai
ATLANTIC
OCEAN
Lake Mweru
ANGOLA
Lubumbashi
ZAMBIA

BURUNDI + RWANDA

UGANDA
Karisimbi
(Volcano)
Byumba
Muramba
Akagera
Gisenyi
Lake
Muhazi
Lake
Ihema
RWANDA
Lake Kivu
Gitarama
Kigali
Lake Mugesera
Kibuye
Nyanza
Lake
Rweru
Kibungo
Mwogo
Cyangugu
Gikongoro
Akanyaru
Kanyaru
Butare
Lake
Cohoha
Muyinga
DEMOCRATIC
REPUBLIC
OF THE
CONGO
Ngozi
Ruvubu
Bubanza
Ruvubu
Muramvya
Bujumbura
Gitega
Ruyigi
BURUNDI
TANZANIA
Lake
Tanganyika
Rutronza
Bururi
Nyanza-Lac

99

TANZANIA

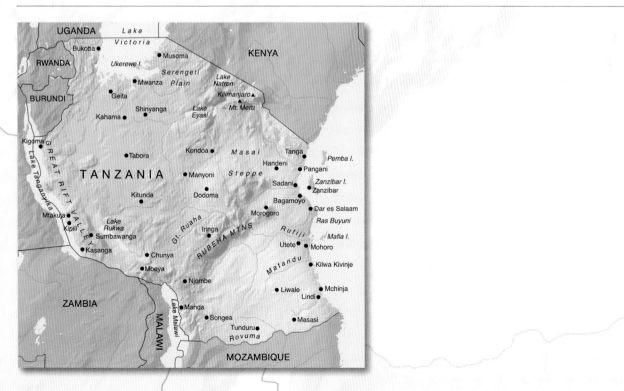

UGANDA
Lake
Victoria
Bukoba
Musoma
KENYA
RWANDA
Ukerewe I.
Serengeti
Plain
Lake
Natron
Mwanza
Kilimanjaro
BURUNDI
Geita
Mt. Meru
Shinyanga
Lake
Eyasi
Kahama
Masai
Kigoma
Tabora
Kondoa
Tanga
Pemba I.
GREAT RIFT VALLEY
Handeni
Pangani
TANZANIA
Manyoni
Steppe
Lake Tanganyika
Sadani
Zanzibar I.
Kitunda
Dodoma
Zanzibar
Bagamoyo
Morogoro
Dar es Salaam
Mtakuja
Gt. Ruaha
Iringa
Ras Buyuni
Lake
Rukwa
Kipili
RUBEHA MTNS
Rufiji
Mafia I.
Sumbawanga
Utete
Mohoro
Kasanga
Chunya
Matandu
Kilwa Kivinje
Mbeya
Njombe
Liwale
Mchinja
Lindi
ZAMBIA
Manda
Songea
Masasi
Lake Malawi
Tunduru
MALAWI
Rovuma
MOZAMBIQUE

ANGOLA

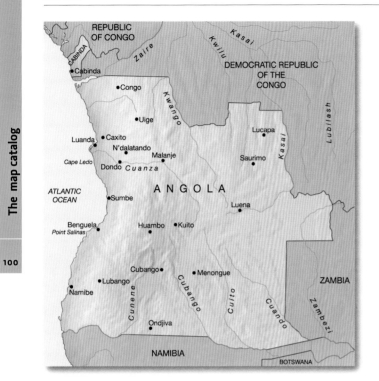

ZAMBIA

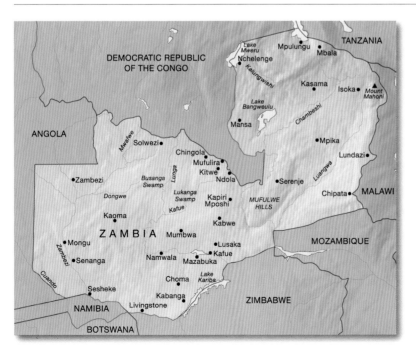

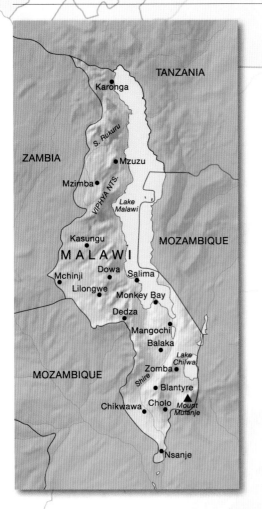

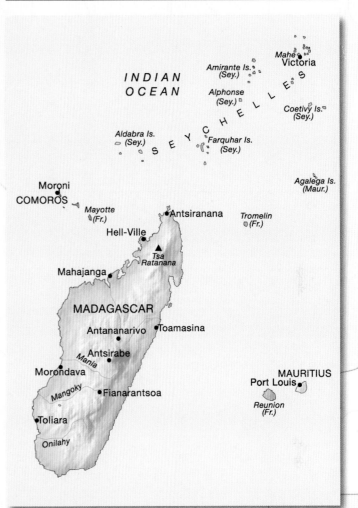

MOZAMBIQUE

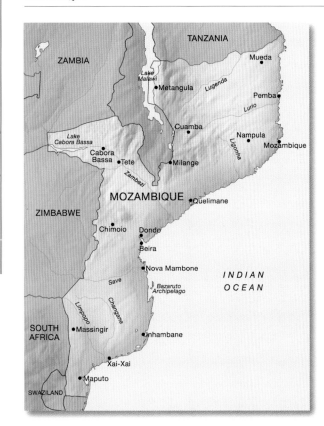

NAMIBIA

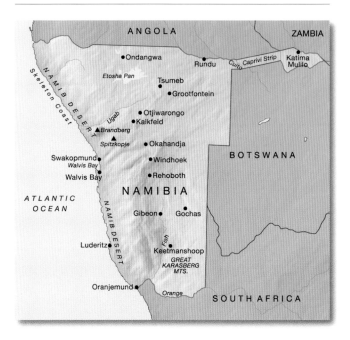

ZIMBABWE

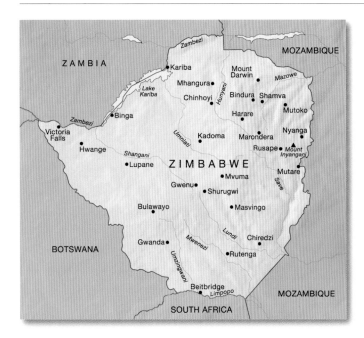

BOTSWANA

ANGOLA

• Shakawe
Kasane

Tsodilo
Hills

Okavango

NAMIBIA

ZIMBABWE

OKAVANGO
DELTA
• Shorobe
• Maun
• Toteng

• Nata

Lake
Ngami

MAKGADIKGADI
PANS

• Ghanzi

Rakops •
Orapa •
Francistown •

B O T S W A N A

Serowe •

• Selebi
Phikwe

Mahalapye •

KALAHARI
DESERT
• Kang

Molepolole •
Gaborone •
• Mochudi

Lobatse •

Tshabong •

S O U T H   A F R I C A

SOUTH AFRICA + LESOTHO + SWAZILAND

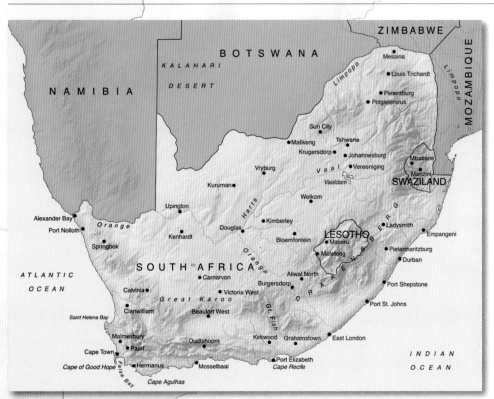

ZIMBABWE

B O T S W A N A

KALAHARI

MOZAMBIQUE

Limpopo

Messina •

N A M I B I A

DESERT

• Louis Trichardt

• Pietersburg
• Potgietersrus

Limpopo

Sun City •

Mafikeng •
Krugersdorp •
Tshwane •

• Johannesburg
• Vereeniging

Mbabane •

Vryburg •

Vaal

Manzini •

SWAZILAND

Kuruman •

Vaaldam

Welkom •

Upington •

Harts

• Kimberley

Alexander Bay •

Orange

Douglas •

Bloemfontein •

Ladysmith •

Empangeni •

Port Nolloth •

Kenhardt •

Springbok •

LESOTHO
Maseru •

Pietermaritzburg •
• Durban

• Mafeteng

D
R
A
K
E
N
S
B
E
R
G

ATLANTIC

S O U T H   A F R I C A

Aliwal North •

OCEAN

• Carnarvon

Burgersdorp •

Port Shepstone •

Calvinia •
• Victoria West

Orange

Gt. Fish

Grahamstown •
East London •

Port St. Johns •

Great Karoo

Clanwilliam •
Beaufort West •

Kirkwood •

Saint Helena Bay

Malmesbury •

Oudtshoorn •

Port Elizabeth •
Cape Recife

INDIAN

Cape Town •
• Paarl

False
Bay

Hermanus •
Mosselbaai •

OCEAN

Cape of Good Hope
Cape Agulhas

RUSSIAN FEDERATION

RUSSIA WEST (TO URALS)

RUSSIA EAST

CHINA

JAPAN

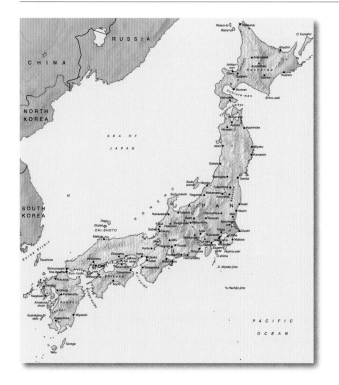

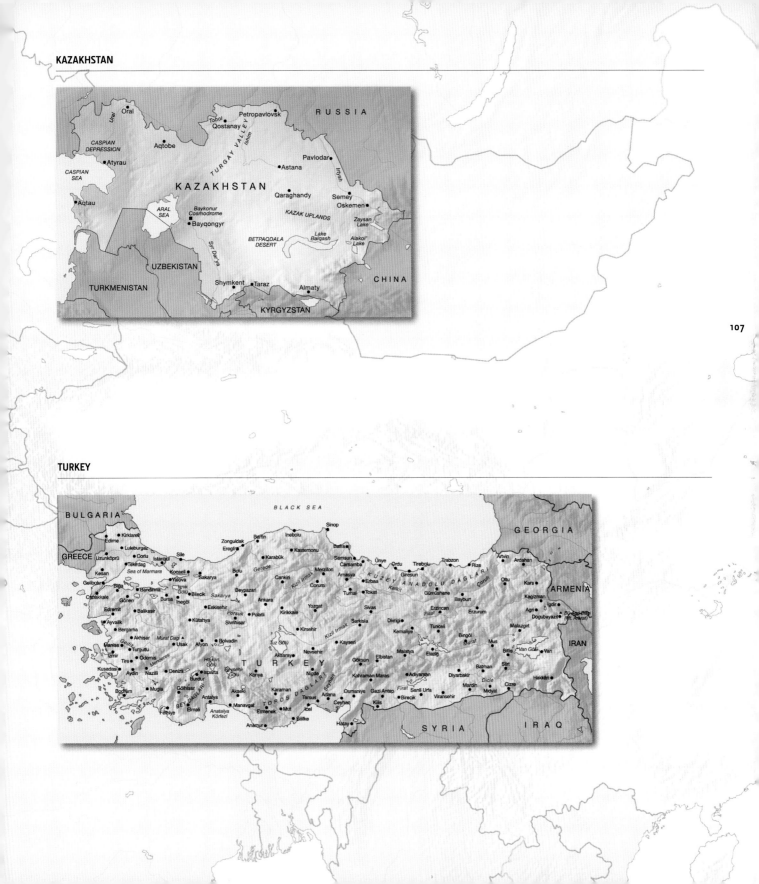

KAZAKHSTAN

RUSSIA

Oral
Tobol
Qostanay
Petropavlovsk

Aqtobe
Pavlodar
TURGAY VALLEY
Ishim
Astana
Irtysh

CASPIAN
DEPRESSION

Atyrau

CASPIAN
SEA

KAZAKHSTAN

Aqtau
Qaraghandy
Semey
Oskemen
KAZAK UPLANDS

ARAL
SEA
Baykonur
Cosmodrome
Bayqongyr
Zaysan
Lake
Alakol'
Lake

Syr Darya
BETPAQDALA
DESERT
Lake
Balqash

UZBEKISTAN

CHINA

TURKMENISTAN
Shymkent
Taraz
Almaty

KYRGYZSTAN

107

TURKEY

BLACK SEA

BULGARIA
GEORGIA

Kırklareli
Edirne
Sinop
Lüleburgaz
Zonguldak
Bartin
İnebolu
Bafra

Uzunköprü
Çorlu
Şile
Ereğli
Kastemonu
Samsun
Ünye
Ordu
Trebolu
Trabzon
Rize
Artvin
Ardahan

GREECE
Keşan
Tekirdağ
İstanbul
Karabük
Gerede
Merzifon
Amasya
KUZEY ANADOLU DAĞLARI
Giresun
Otlu
Kars

Gelibolu
Kocaeli
Sakarya
Bolu
Çankırı
Çorum
Erbaa
Tokat
Kelkit
Gümüşhane
Çoruh
Kağızman
İğdır

Biga
Bandırma
Yalova
İznik Gölü
Sakarya
Beypazarı
Ankara
Kızıl Irmak
Turhal
Bayburt
Erzurum
ARMENIA

Çanakkale
Gönen
Bursa
İnegöl
Bilecik
Eskişehir
Polatlı
Yozgat
Sivas
Erzincan
Fırat
Tunceli
Ağrı
Büyük Ağrı Dağı
(Mt. Ararat)
Doğubayazıt

Edremit
Balıkesir
Kütahya
Porsuk
Sıvrıhisar
Kırıkkale
Şarkışla
Divriği
Kemaliye
Bingöl
Muş
Malazgirt

Ayvalık
Akhisar
Murat Dağı
Uşak
Afyon
Bolvadin
Kırşehir
Kayseri
Murat
Van Gölü

Bergama
Gediz
Turgutlu
Kızıl Irmak
Tunceli
Elazığ
Bitlis
Van

Manisa
Tire
Ödemiş
Menderes
Nazilli
Tuz Gölü
Nevşehir
Göksun
Elbistan
Malatya
IRAN

İzmir
Aydın
Denizli
Isparta
Aksaray
Niğde
Kahraman Maraş
Adıyaman
Diyarbakır
Batman
Siirt
Hakkari

Kuşadası
Muğla
Burdur
Eğridir Gölü
Konya
Karaman
TOROS DAĞLARI
Tarsus
Adana
Osmaniye
Gazi Antep
Şanlı Urfa
Mardin
Dicle
Midyat
Cizre

Bodrum
Göltbaşı
Antalya
Akseki
Seyhan
Ceyhan
Kilis
Birecik
Viranşehir

Fethiye
Elmalı
Manavgat
Ermenek
Mut
İçel
Silifke
Hatay

Anatalya Körfezi
Anamur

TURKEY

SYRIA
IRAQ

MONGOLIA

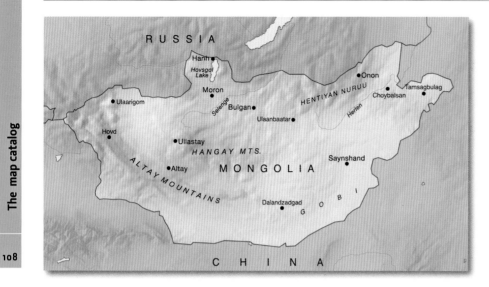

TURKMENISTAN + UZBEKISTAN

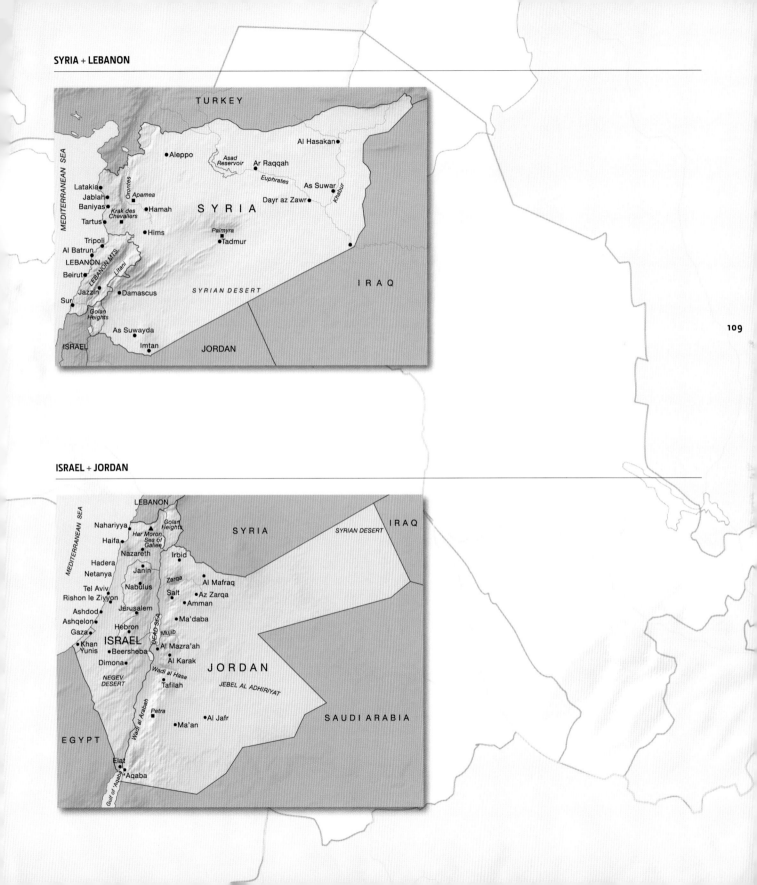

TURKEY

SYRIA

MEDITERRANEAN SEA

Aleppo
Al Hasakan
Asad Reservoir
Ar Raqqah
Euphrates
As Suwar
Latakia
Jablah
Orontes
Apamea
Baniyas
Krak des Chevaliers
Hamah
Dayr az Zawr
Khabur
Tartus
Hims
Palmyra
Tripoli
Tadmur
Al Batrun
LEBANON
LEBANON MTS.
Litani
Beirut
IRAQ
Jazzin
SYRIAN DESERT
Damascus
Sur
Golan Heights
As Suwayda
ISRAEL
Imtan
JORDAN

109

LEBANON

MEDITERRANEAN SEA

Nahariyya
Golan Heights
SYRIA
IRAQ
SYRIAN DESERT
Haifa
Har Moron
Sea of Galilee
Nazareth
Irbid
Hadera
Janin
Netanya
Zarqa
Al Mafraq
Tel Aviv
Nabulus
Salt
Az Zarqa
Rishon le Ziyyon
Jerusalem
Amman
Ashdod
Ma'daba
Ashqelon
Hebron
DEAD SEA
Gaza
Mujib
Khan Yunis
ISRAEL
Al Mazra'ah
Beersheba
Al Karak
Dimona
JORDAN
NEGEV DESERT
Wadi al Hasa
Tafilah
JEBEL AL ADHIRIYAT
Wadi al Arabah
Petra
Ma'an
Al Jafr
SAUDI ARABIA
EGYPT
Elat
Aqaba
Gulf of 'Aqaba

KOREA (NORTH)

KOREA (SOUTH)

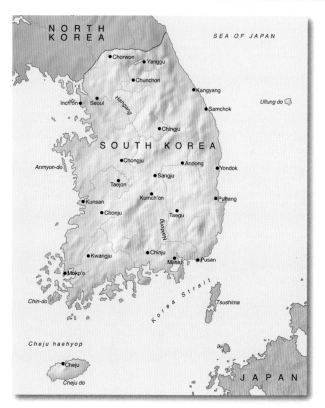

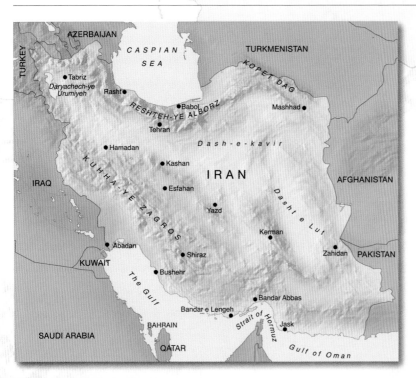

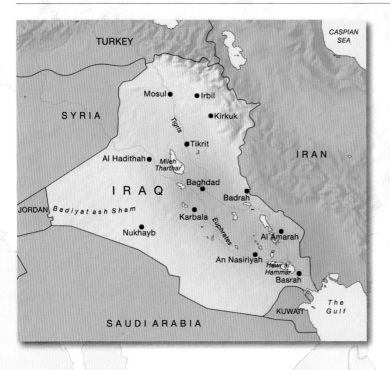

SAUDI ARABIA + KUWAIT

KYRGYZSTAN + TAJIKISTAN

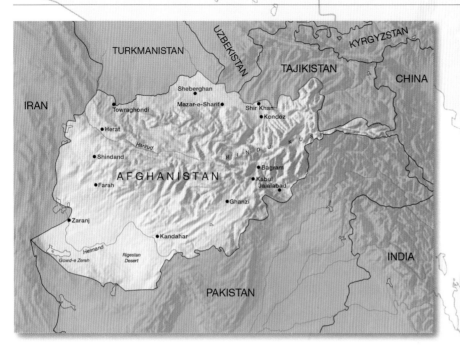

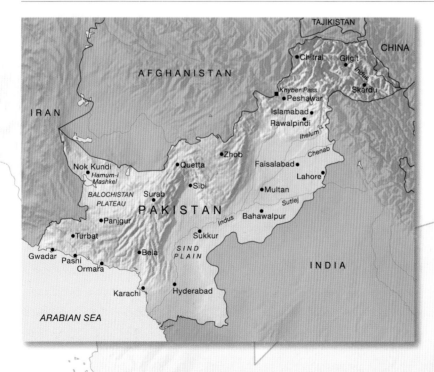

INDIA + SRI LANKA + MALDIVES

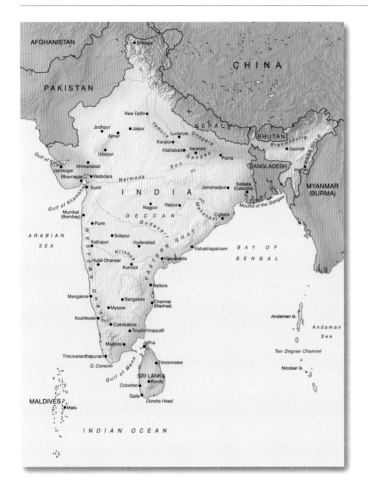

BAHRAIN + UAE + QATAR

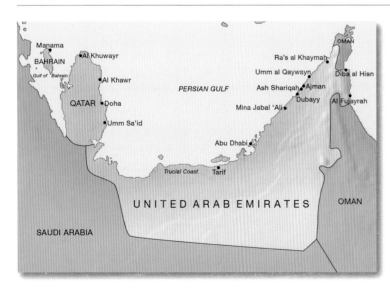

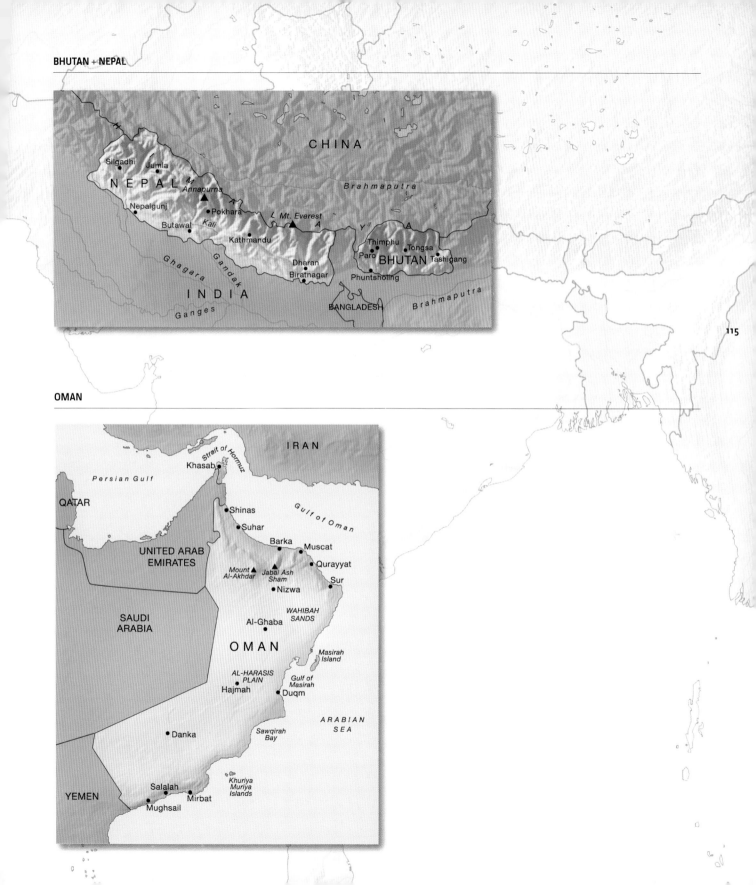

BHUTAN + NEPAL map

CHINA

NEPAL

Silgadhi

Jumla

Annapurna

Nepalgunj

Pokhara

Butawal

Kali

Kathmandu

Mt. Everest

Brahmaputra

Thimphu

Tongsa

Paro

BHUTAN

Tashigang

Dharan

Biratnagar

Phuntsholing

Ghagara

Gandak

INDIA

Ganges

BANGLADESH

Brahmaputra

OMAN map

IRAN

Strait of Hormuz

Khasab

Persian Gulf

QATAR

Gulf of Oman

Shinas

Suhar

UNITED ARAB
EMIRATES

Barka

Muscat

Mount
Al-Akhdar

Jabal Ash
Sham

Qurayyat

Nizwa

Sur

SAUDI
ARABIA

WAHIBAH
SANDS

Al-Ghaba

OMAN

Masirah
Island

AL-HARASIS
PLAIN

Gulf of
Masirah

Hajmah

Duqm

ARABIAN
SEA

Danka

Sawqirah
Bay

Khuriya
Muriya
Islands

Salalah

YEMEN

Mirbat

Mughsail

YEMEN

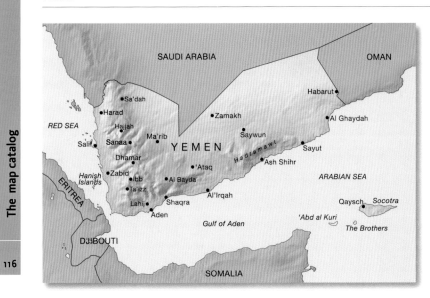

BANGLADESH

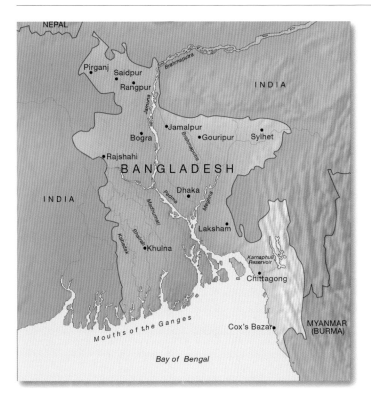

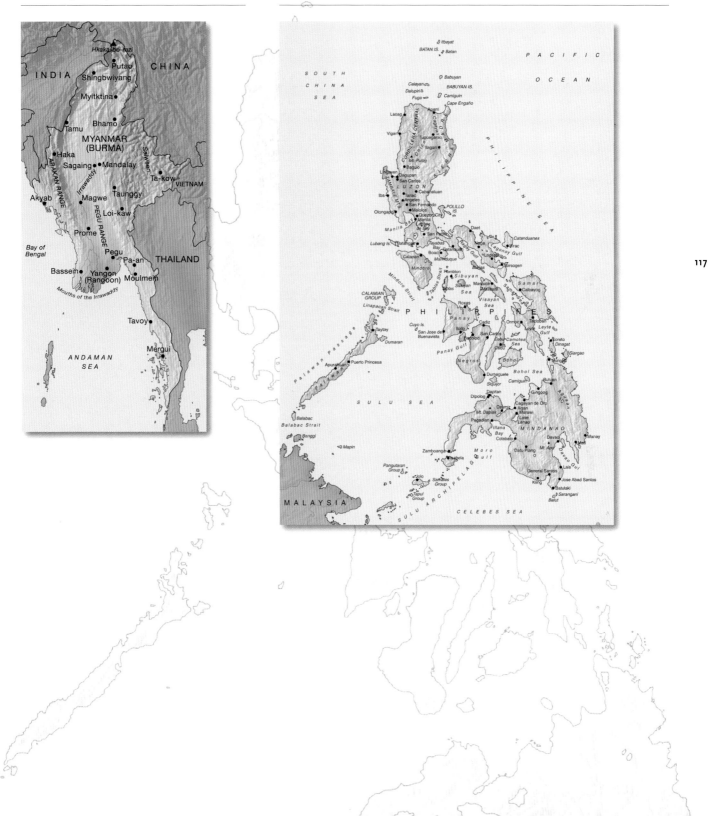

VIETNAM

CHINA

Lai Chau
Red
Black
Lang Son
Hanoi
Son La
Hoa
Binh
Nam Dinh

*Gulf of
Tonkin*

LAOS

Ku Son

Vinh

Dong Hoi

Bong Ha

Da Nang

*SOUTH
CHINA
SEA*

THAILAND

VIETNAM

Quy Nhon
Pleiku
Tuy Hoa
Nha
Trang
CAMBODIA
Da Lai
Cam
Ranh
Mekong
Loc Ninh
Phan
Thiet
Ho Chi Minh City

*Gulf of
Thailand*

Tra Vinh
*Dao Phu
Quoc*
Rach
Gia
Con Dao

LAOS

CHINA

Phongsali

*MYANMAR
(BURMA)*
Louang
Namtha
Xam Nua

VIETNAM

*GULF OF
TONKIN*

Mekong
Louangphrabang

Xiangkhoang

L A O S ▲ Phu Bia

Ban Nape

Vientiane

Mekong

Muang
Khammouan

Savannakhet

THAILAND

Saravan

Pakxe

CAMBODIA

THAILAND

*MYANMAR
(BURMA)*

LAOS

VIETNAM

*Gulf
of
Tonkin*

Chiang
Mai
Nan

DAWNA RANGE

Phrae

Udon Thani

Mekong

ping

Tak
T H A I L A N D
Chi
Phichit

Udon Ratchathani

Chai Nat

Mun

Lop Buri

PHANOM DANG RAEK MTS.

Nam Tok
Aranyaprathet
Bangkok

CAMBODIA

*ANDAMAN
SEA*

Sattahip
Trat
Ko Chang
Prachuap
Khiri Khan
Ko Kut

Chumphon

*Gulf
of
Thailand*

Ranong
Ko Phangan
Ko Samui
Surat Thani

Takua Pa

Phuket
Trang
Songkhla

*Strait
of
Malacca*

MALAYSIA

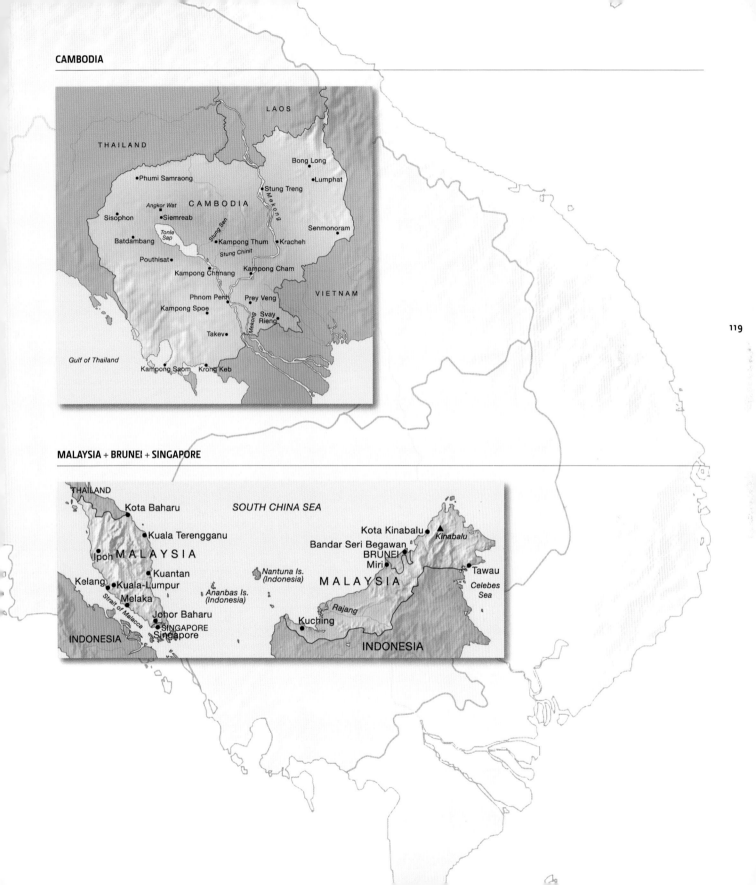

CAMBODIA

LAOS

THAILAND

Bong Long
• Lumphat

• Phumi Samraong

• Stung Treng

Angkor Wat
CAMBODIA

Sisophon •
• Siemreab

Stung Sen

Senmonoram

Tonle Sap
Batdambang •
• Kampong Thum
• Kracheh

Pouthisat •
Stung Chinit

Kampong Chhnang •
• Kampong Cham

VIETNAM

Phnom Penh •
• Prey Veng

Kampong Spoe •
Mekong
Svay
Rieng

Takev •

Gulf of Thailand

Kampong Saom •
• Krong Keb

119

MALAYSIA + BRUNEI + SINGAPORE

THAILAND

Kota Baharu •
SOUTH CHINA SEA

• Kuala Terengganu

Kota Kinabalu •
▲ *Kinabalu*

Bandar Seri Begawan •

Ipoh • MALAYSIA

BRUNEI
Miri •

• Kuantan

*Nantuna Is.
(Indonesia)*

MALAYSIA

Tawau •

Kelang •
Kuala-Lumpur •

*Ananbas Is.
(Indonesia)*

*Celebes
Sea*

Melaka •

Rajang

Strait of Malacca

Johor Baharu •

Kuching •

• SINGAPORE
Singapore •

INDONESIA

INDONESIA

MICRONESIA + PALAU + NAURU + MARSHALL ISLANDS

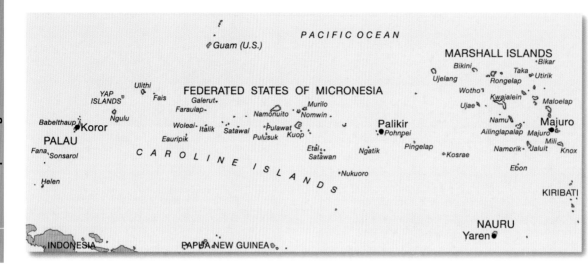

INDONESIA + EAST TIMOR

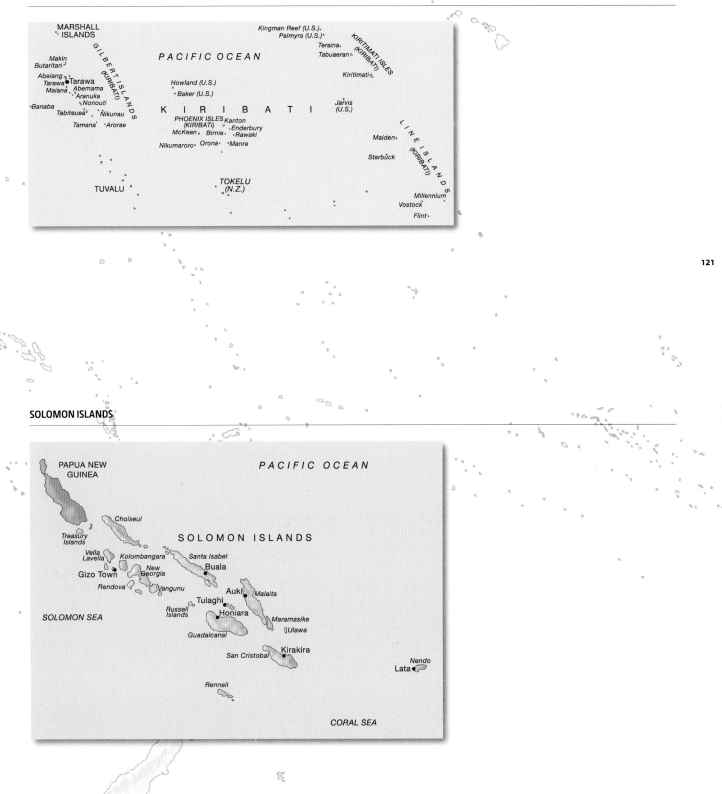

PAPUA NEW GUINEA

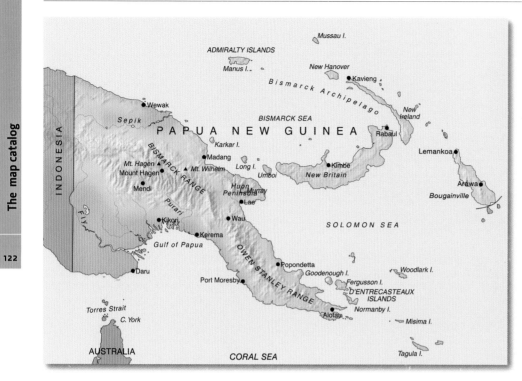

AUSTRALIA WEST

AUSTRALIA EAST

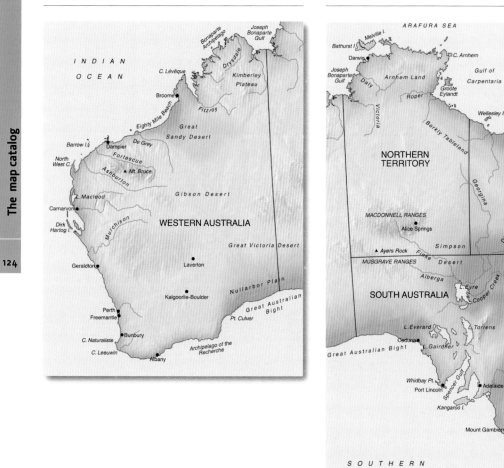

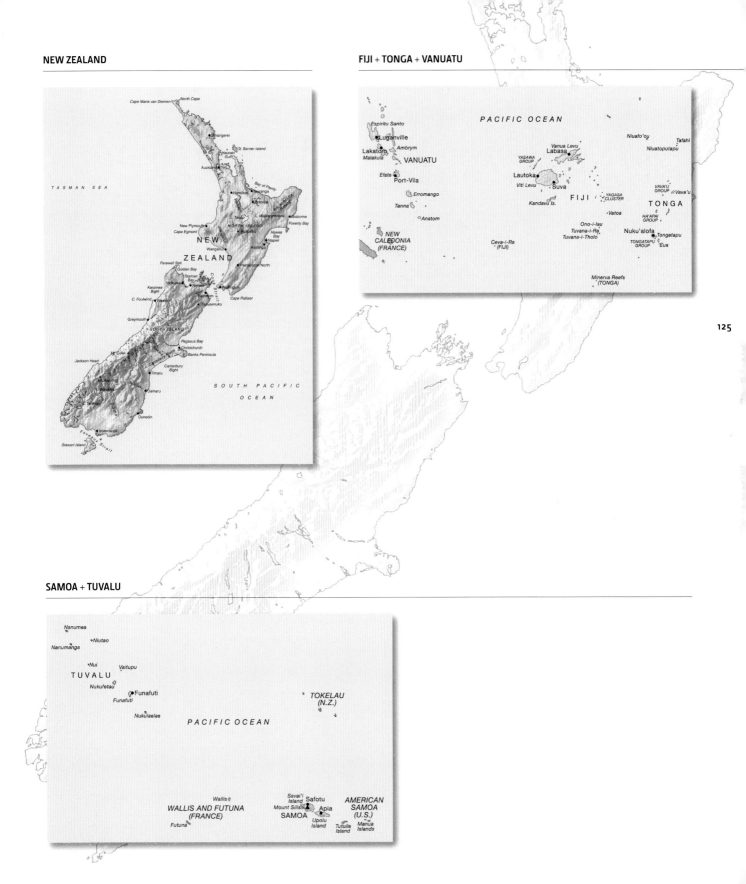

NEW ZEALAND

Cape Maria van Diemen
North Cape
Whangarei
Gt. Barrier Island
Hauraki
Gulf
Auckland
Hamilton
Tauranga
Bay of Plenty
Rotorua
TASMAN SEA
Taupo
Gisborne
L. Waikaremoana
Poverty Bay
New Plymouth
NORTH ISLAND
Cape Egmont
Ruapehu
Hawke
Bay
Napier
NEW
Hastings
Wanganui
ZEALAND
Palmerston North
Farewell Spit
Golden Bay
Tasman
Bay
Nelson
Karamea
Bight
Motueka
Wellington
C. Foulwind
Westport
Blenheim
Cape Palliser
Kaikoura
Greymouth
SOUTH ISLAND
Pegasus Bay
Mt. Cook
Christchurch
Banks Peninsula
Jackson Head
Canterbury
Bight
Timaru
SOUTH PACIFIC
Mt Aspiring
Oamaru
OCEAN
Wanaka
Wakatipu
Te Anau
Dunedin
Invercargill
Foveaux Strait
Stewart Island

FIJI + TONGA + VANUATU

PACIFIC OCEAN
Espiritu Santo
Luganville
Niuafo'ou
Tafahi
Ambrym
Vanua Levu
Niuatoputapu
Lakatoro
Labasa
Malakula
VANUATU
YASAWA
GROUP
Efate
Port-Vila
Lautoka
VAVA'U
GROUP
Vava'u
Viti Levu
Suva
Erromango
FIJI
YAGASA
CLUSTER
TONGA
Tanna
Kandavu Is.
Vatoa
HA'APAI
GROUP
Anatom
Ono-i-lau
Nuku'alofa
Tongatapu
NEW
Tuvana-i-Ra
TONGATAPU
Eua
CALEDONIA
Ceva-i-Ra
Tuvana-i-Tholo
GROUP
(FRANCE)
(FIJI)
Minerva Reefs
(TONGA)

125

SAMOA + TUVALU

Nanumea
Niutao
Nanumanga
Nui
Vaitupu
TUVALU
Nukufetau
Funafuti
TOKELAU
Funafuti
(N.Z.)
Nukulaelae
PACIFIC OCEAN
Wallis
Savai'i
Island
Safotu
AMERICAN
WALLIS AND FUTUNA
Mount Silisili
Apia
SAMOA
(FRANCE)
SAMOA
(U.S.)
Futuna
Upolu
Island
Tutuila
Island
Manua
Islands

Glossary

Adjustment layer

A specialized layer that can be handled as a conventional layer, but designed to enact effects on layers below it in the image "stack." These include changes to levels, contrast, and color, plus gradients and other effects. These changes do not permanently affect the pixels underneath, so by masking or removing the adjustment layer, you can easily remove the effect from part or all of an image with great ease. You can also returnand change the parameters of an adjustment layer at a later stage.

Blending mode

In Photoshop Elements, individual layers can be blended with those underneath, rather than simply overlaying them at full opacity. Blending modes control the ways in which the layers interact, enacting changes on one layer using the color information in the other. The result is a new color based on the original color and the nature of the blend.

Contrast

The degree of difference between adjacent tones in an image, from the lightest to the darkest.

Curves

A Photoshop tool for precise control of tonal relationships, contrast, and color.

Drag

To move an item or selection across the screen, by clicking and holding the cursor over it, then moving the mouse with the button still pressed.

Eyedropper

A tool used to define the foreground and background colors in the Tools palette, either by clicking on colors that appear in an image, or in a specific color palette dialog box. Eyedroppers are also used to sample colors for Levels, Curves, and Color Range processes.

Feather

An option used to soften the edge of a selection that has been moved or otherwise manipulated, in order to hide the seams between the selected area and the pixels that surround it.

Fill

A Photoshop operation which covers a defined area with a particular color, gradient, texture, or pattern.

Graphics tablet

A drawing device consisting of a stylus and a pressure-sensitive tablet. Many people find them easier to use than mice for drawing. The pressure sensitivity can be set to different functions, such as controlling the opacity of an eraser, or the width of a brush.

Grayscale

An image or gradient made up of a series of 256 gray tones covering the entire gamut between black and white.

Halftone

A technique of reproducing a continuous tone image on a printing press by breaking it up into a pattern of equally spaced dots of varying size. The larger the dots used by the halftone pattern, the darker the shade.

Handle

An icon used in image-editing applications to manipulate a selection. These usually appear as small black squares that can be moved by clicking and dragging with the mouse.

Hard light

A blending mode that creates an effect similar to directing a bright light on the subject, emphasizing contrast and exaggerating highlights.

Layer

A feature used to produce composite images by suspending image elements on separate overlays. Once these layers have been created, they can be re-ordered, blended, and their transparency (opacity) may be altered.

Layer styles

A series of useful preset effects that can be applied to the contents of a layer. Examples include drop shadows, embossing, and color tone effects.

Layer mask

A mask that can be applied to elements of an image in a particular layer, defining which pixels will or will not be visible or affect pixels underneath.

Multiply

A blending mode that uses the pixels of one layer to multiply those below. The resulting color is always darker, except where white appears on an upper layer.

Opacity

In a layered Photoshop Elements document, the degree of transparency that each layer of an image has in relation to the layer beneath. As the opacity is lowered, the layer beneath shows through.

Overlay

A blending mode that retains black and white in their original forms, but darkens dark areas and lightens light areas.

Pen tool

A tool used for drawing vector paths in Photoshop Elements.

PPI Pixels per inch.

The most common unit of resolution, describing how many pixels are contained within a single linear inch of an image.

Quick Mask

A feature designed to rapidly create a mask around a selection. By switching to Quick Mask mode, the user can paint and erase the mask using simple brushstrokes.

Resolution

In digital images, the resolution is normally given as pixels per inch (PPI). Images for printing are usually 150-300ppi, and those for screen display, 72ppi.

Vector Path

A shape that is generated using paths (or an illustration program such as Adobe Illustrator) that is not pixel-dependent. As a result, a vector can be resized without a loss of quality.

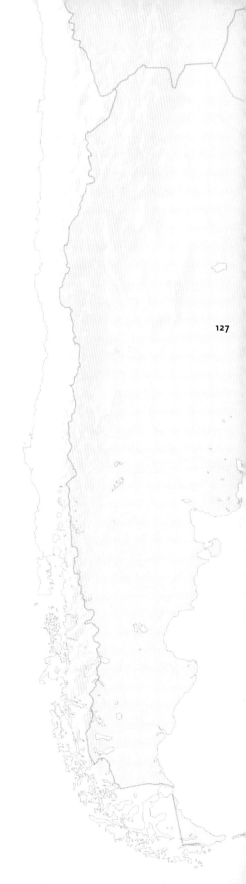